T0107432

Creating a Hostile Environment for the Flesh

Reclaiming and Maintaining Personal Victory

Pastor Bernard King

WESTBOW
P R E S S
A DIVISION OF THOMAS NELSON

WestBow Press books may be ordered through booksellers or by contacting:

WestBow Press
A Division of Thomas Nelson
1663 Liberty Drive
Bloomington, IN 47403
www.westbowpress.com
1-(866) 928-1240

ISBN: 978-1-4908-0651-8 (sc)
ISBN: 978-1-4908-0652-5 (e)

Library of Congress Control Number: 2013915405

Printed in the United States of America.

WestBow Press rev. date: 10/28/2013

Table of Contents

Thanks and Appreciation

I would like to take this opportunity to thank our God and Father for His goodness and mercy that is ministered unto me every morning and follows me all the days of my life. I thank my splendid soul mate and helper from heaven, Gloria, whose love, support, encouragement, and belief in me is immeasurable. I thank my three sons, Bernard Jr., Philip, and Seth, for their prayers and lives that reveal a love for the Lord. I thank Dr. Lina Paske for her heaven-sent persistence, patience, and precious outpouring of time and sacrifice. I also want to thank God's incredible, separated-to-the-gospel servants at Cornerstone Bible Fellowship. May God richly reward your uncompromising devotion, service, and loyalty to Him, and your love and loyalty for this piece of clay you affectionately affirm as your pastor.

FtGG
For the Glory of God

Pastor Bernard King sr.

Introduction

The basis of this book was birthed while I was busy engaging in a routine fitness regime (temple maintenance). I had completed my upper body and cardio exercises, so I was deliberately determined to go after my abdominals (wishing for washboards). After ripping out repetition after repetition of crunches and leg raises, my upper and lower abdominal muscles began to respond to the aggravated assault by sending their usual SOS signal to my mental headquarters.

As I seriously considered answering their cries of anguish and capitulating to their convincing case, an epiphany entered my mind. It was a divine disclosure that directed me to an awesome analogy and a laudable lesson with respect to the differences between spiritual and personal victory versus spiritual and personal defeat.

An Unwanted Intruder

For I know that in me [that is, in my flesh] dwelleth no good thing. Romans 7:18a KJV

When my oldest son, BJ, was in high school, we paid a visit to the dermatologist to address an aggressive wart that had staked its claim on the side of his face near his left temple.

After analyzing and assessing my son's dermatological issue, the dermatologist recommended three different approaches of treatment for this tenacious and troubling intruder: We could try to lance or cut the wart off. We could try to freeze it off, or we could try to treat it topically with a solution or cream. The first two options would probably leave a scar, so we elected to treat the intruder topically.

The objective was to create a hostile environment for the wart. This would not only remove it but also revoke the wart's encroachment. It will also eradicate its ruling influence and reclaim and maintain BJ's healthy and handsome appearance.

Similarly, in order for us to become devoted disciples of the Lord Jesus Christ, we must be deliberate and determined to develop a discipline that will deliver us from the demands of our sinful nature.

My son experienced an unwanted intruder that was external. It was easily detectable. The unwanted intruder that I deliberately want to expose and exterminate is not external, but rather internal. It demands a solution that will not come from human resources, science, education, or medicine.

The pathology of this profound, persistent perpetrator originated in the very first beings that existed, whose origin and history is accurately recorded in the Word of God (the Holy Scriptures). Sin is the unwanted intruder that has invaded our lives and sentenced the whole world to eternal separation from God (eternal death) "Wherefore, as by one man sin entered into the world, and death by sin; and so death passed upon all men, for that all have sinned: Romans 5:12 KJV

It is because of this eternal truth that we must endeavor to create a hostile environment in our hearts and minds that will remove the rampant and ruling influence of the flesh (willful and sinful nature) in our lives. Furthermore, we must secure sound steps to stamp out any suggestive and subversive advances in our attitudes that consequently incarcerate our minds and hearts in a habitual, profound pity and personal defeat.

This book is written for the willing and humble of hearts who are seeking to enjoy a life of consistent change and victory. I believe that a robust spiritual skill set will reward you with a rich and intimate relationship with the Lord Jesus Christ.

It is my prayer that God, by His amazing grace, will cause you to internalize and apply the material mentioned in this book in order that you will abandon defeat and start on the stairs of victory. So, Lord willing, let's proceed and procure the following steps that will forward your success in creating a hostile environment for the flesh, which will maintain and reclaim personal victory.

CHAPTER 1

Reevaluating Your Power Resource

The Lord is my strength and song, and he is
become my salvation. …
Thy right hand, O Lord is become glorious in power.
Exodus 15:2a, 6a KJV

Before you start this journey of personal victory, it is important that you consider what I believe to be an essential prerequisite that will empower and point you to strength, personal victory, and eternal victory that only the hand and power of God can give.

Moses is widely regarded as one of the most revered and recognized prophets and leaders in Hebrew history. God in His matchless mercy and prodigious providence empowered and strengthened His servant Moses. God placed him in a position to liberate the children of Israel from the suffocating and severe servitude that strangled and swallowed the children of Israel for more than four hundred years. I propose to you that Moses witnessed, walked, and worked in the strength and power of God.

In Exodus 15, Moses wrote a song that I believe conveys a concrete truth. That is, human strength or willpower is sorely inadequate to conquer and catapult us over the most complex, challenging, and crippling crises in our lives.

The children of Israel experienced a majestic and miraculous victory over their enemy. The Egyptians envisioned the Israelite's extermination at the banks of the Red Sea. However, their anticipation of victory was vanquished when the hand of God choked out their cries of conquest and routed them with the Red Sea.

When the Israelites witnessed the massive number of Egyptian soldier's lifeless bodies wash ashore, they went right into praise mode. The mouths of Moses and the children of Israel were moved to minister to their God in song.

"Then sang Moses and the children of Israel this song unto the LORD, and spake, saying, I will sing unto the LORD, for he hath triumphed gloriously: the horse and his rider hath he thrown into the sea. The LORD is my *strength* and song, and he is become my *salvation*: he is my God, and I will prepare him an habitation; my father's God, and I will exalt him. The LORD is a man of war: the LORD is his name. Pharaoh's chariots and his host hath he cast into the sea: his chosen captains also are drowned in the Red sea. The depths have covered them: they sank into the bottom as a stone. Thy right *hand*, O LORD, is become glorious in *power*: thy right hand, O LORD, hath dashed in pieces the enemy.' Exodus 15:1-6, KJV emphasis added

Notice that Moses and the children of Israel did not sing about their capacity to will or deliver themselves out of the hands of the enemy. They sang that God was their strength and their song. Therefore, it's imperative to Promote and trust the power of God and His strength as your resource and not your personal willpower. However, you cannot employ what is nonexistent, and you cannot engage on empty! You need the power of God—*God's* power as opposed to your personal willpower.

In addition, I submit to you that personal willpower is a resource that is reserved for those who renounce and remove themselves from the resurrecting power of God. Have you ever asked yourself, "How much power did God employ to raise the dead? Is that power available to those who trust Him as their Lord and God?" Absolutely!

The apostle Paul prayed a very personal, profound, and powerful prayer, asking God to assist the believers at Ephesus in trusting God and positioning themselves in his mighty power of God. Look at and lock your mind and heart on the apostle's announcement and assessment of the awesome power of God.

And what is the exceeding greatness of his power to us-ward who believe, according to the working of his mighty power, which he wrought in Christ, when he raised him from the dead, and set him at his own right hand in the heavenly places. Ephesians 1:19-20 KJV

When you engage in personal willpower, you substitute the very power that raised our Lord Jesus Christ from the grave with your independence from God. And independence from God will never place you in a position of strength and victory in your spiritual life.

Independence from God is the height of indifference and immediate impotency! Remember, the Word of God adamantly announces that apart from God we cannot accomplish anything. Conversely, with God *all* things are possible! Therefore, the reality of the resurrected power of Christ must be in your life. Furthermore, we must be profoundly persuaded by the person and power of Jesus Christ. I believe that before we can commence toward the path of conquest, *we must be conquered by Christ.*

Is the resurrecting power of Jesus Christ a reality in your life? If you cannot answer that question in the absolute affirmative, it is important for you to purposely ponder and process the following information because eternal ramifications are at stake here.

The catalyst for genuine and profound change that promotes the purposes of God and the glory of God in our lives begins with securing and submitting to His truth versus suppressing His truth! The source of truth, the strength of truth, and the supremacy of truth, is situated with God and His Word.

And the LORD passed by before him, and proclaimed, The LORD, The LORD God, merciful and gracious, longsuffering, and abundant in goodness and *truth*. Exodus 34:6, KJV emphasis added

He is the Rock, his work [is] perfect: for all his ways are judgment: a God of *truth* and without iniquity, just and right is he. Deuteronomy 32:4, KJV emphasis added

Thy righteousness is an everlasting righteousness, and thy law [is] the *truth*. Psalms 119:142, KJV emphasis added

I pray that the aforementioned passages, with respect to God's truth, have placed your heart in a position of humility that will help you handle the truth. Here is the truth regarding our humanity's absolute need of redemption and healing!

It is the Word of God (the Holy Scriptures) and the power of His Spirit that will convict your conscience and capture your heart with respect to your spiritual position with God. And that spiritual position is that you are separated from God due to your sinful condition, and He will not hear you until you repent and call on His name for salvation and forgiveness for your sins: "But your iniquities have separated between you and your God, and your sins have hid [his] face from you, that he will not hear" Isaiah 59:2. KJV

Furthermore apart from God's influence and authority in our lives, you are subjected and seduced by an innate rebellion which leads to indifference toward the will and purposes of God. The Scriptures emphatically declare that this deliberate disposition is sin. Sin is a transgression (breaking or violating) against the law of God: "Whosoever committeth sin transgresseth also the law: for sin is the transgression of the law" 1 John 3:4. KJV

The Word of God has also concluded that universally every soul that has ever existed in the past and in the present is severely separated from God because of our sinful position: "For all have sinned, and come short of the glory of God" Romans 3:23 KJV

Notice the text states *all* of us, including this author, have sinned against God. Now before you object and protest this point and park in your personal piety and pride, and before you begin to promote and present your membership card of your denominational choice and trumpet your treatise of tradition, permit me to refer you to the Bible's M.R.I.(Masters resonance imaging)

The Word of God (the Holy Scriptures) will accurately reveal an absolute picture and impeccable image of the problem (sin) in every person's heart. God has said that His Word is a lamp unto our feet and a light unto our path Psalm 119:105. KJV So let's shine His light on the issue of the sin of self-righteousness.

In the book of Exodus chapter 20, God gives us His Ten Commandments (and not ten casual considerations). God's commandments will consistently deliver a crippling and crushing blow to our consciences of conceit. This is essential in creating the condition of our heart and minds that will move us from self-righteousness to His righteousness.

"I [am] the LORD thy God, which have brought thee out of the land of Egypt, out of the house of bondage. Thou shalt have no other gods before me. Thou shalt not make unto thee any graven image, or any likeness [of anything] that [is] in heaven above, or that [is] in the earth beneath, or that [is] in the water under the earth:

Thou shalt not bow down thyself to them, nor serve them: for I the LORD thy God [am] a jealous God, visiting the iniquity of the fathers upon the children unto the third and fourth [generation] of them that hate me; And shewing mercy unto thousands of them that love me, and keep my commandments. Thou shalt not take the name of the LORD thy God in vain; for the LORD will not hold him guiltless that taketh his name in vain. Remember the Sabbath day, to keep it holy. Six days shalt thou labour, and do all thy work:

But the seventh day [is] the Sabbath of the LORD thy God: [in it] thou shalt not do any work, thou, nor thy son, nor thy daughter, thy manservant, nor thy maidservant, nor thy cattle, nor thy stranger that [is] within thy gates: For [in] six days the LORD made heaven and earth, the sea, and all that in them [is], and rested the seventh day: wherefore the LORD blessed the Sabbath day, and hallowed it.

Honour thy father and thy mother: that thy days may be long upon the land which the LORD thy God giveth thee. Thou shalt not kill. Thou shalt not commit adultery. Thou shalt not steal. Thou shalt not bear false witness against thy neighbour. Thou shalt not covet thy neighbour's house, thou shalt not covet thy neighbour's wife, nor his manservant, nor his maidservant, nor his ox, nor his ass, nor any thing that [is] thy neighbour's." Exodus 20:1-17 KJV

With absolute certainty, I offer to you that all of humanity has transgressed or broken all of the ten commandments at least once, but most likely multiple times in one's life.

You may protest, "I have not personally murdered anyone or committed adultery!" Well I ask you to consider how many times have you murdered your employer or an-in-law or competitor in your heart and mind? The Lord Jesus Christ who is the only perfect man and flawless individual that ever lived also laid out the truth that if we have lusted or desired a woman who did not belong to us by way of marriage, we have committed adultery in our hearts. This is also true in the case of a woman desiring a man who does not belong to her: "But I say unto you, That whosoever looketh on a woman to lust after her hath committed *adultery* with her already in his *heart*" Matthew 5:28, KJV emphasis added).

Therefore we must turn our opposition to the truth regarding our sinful condition obsolete in light of the Word. Furthermore, according to the law of God, idolaters, blasphemers, Sabbath breakers, those who are dishonorable to their parents, murderers, adulterers, thieves, liars, and the covetous are an offense to God and thereby will not be permitted to go to heaven. If you break any of the laws of God just once, you are guilty: "For whosoever shall keep the whole law, and yet offend in one [point], he is guilty of all" James 2:10.KJV

Remember, all of us have sinned. That is the truth about our *condemnation* but don't leave until you have read about our *salvation, restoration, emancipation,* and *reconciliation,* which will lead us to *celebration*!

Because of your separation, you are currently in a position that automatically comes with a penalty: *death*. "For the wages of sin is death" Romans 6:23a.KJV

Now that we know the truth about the bad news, I would like to present the good news!

God, by His divine providence and immeasurable grace, produced the perfect provision for the forgiveness and penalty for our sins. He delivered up His dearly and deeply loved Son as an immaculate and absolutely impeccable sacrifice. With His Son's death, He purchased our redemption (God's action for saving us from sin) and secured our salvation with His life!

For God so loved the world, that he gave his only begotten Son, that whosoever believeth in him should not perish, but have everlasting life. John 3:16 KJV

In whom we have redemption through his blood, even the forgiveness of sins. Colossians 1:14 KJV

"Forasmuch as ye know that ye were not redeemed with corruptible things, as silver and gold, from your vain conversation received by tradition from your fathers; But with the precious blood of Christ, as of a lamb without blemish and without spot." 1 Peter 1:18-19 KJV

Therefore you must personally trust by *faith* in the transcendent and incomparable conquest and provision on the cross of Christ Jesus the Lord. It is only when we repent, receive, and respond to the gospel that we secure eternal life.

The gospel is the death, burial, and resurrection (DBR) of Jesus Christ. That is what countless number of souls rest and refer to as the "good news." The good news is that God has graciously granted us eternal life and the forgiveness of sins when He offered up His Son as the perfect sacrifice and thereby delivered us from the penalty of sin which is eternal separation from God: "But the gift of God is eternal life through Jesus Christ our Lord" Romans 6:23b. KJV

Repentance is characterized by one's change of mind, change of heart, and change of will. This will translate to you making a U-turn and allowing His *rightful* turn in your life. His divine power (the Holy Spirit) will give you the capacity to conquer, resist, and renounce your former rebellion. The Word of God decisively declares: Knowing this, that our old man is crucified with him, that the body of sin might be destroyed, that henceforth we should not serve sin. Romans 6:6 KJV

If you have come to that place in your mind and heart where you unequivocally embrace and believe that you are a sinner and you completely understand that there is a penalty and punishment for your sins.

God provided His Son Jesus to answer the penalty and receive the punishment for your sins. Are you courageously willing to repent and place your trust in God's absolute provision for your sins?

So as a former beggar who was blistered and bruised in heart and mind, bewildered about life and enslaved by conceit and foolish passions. I realized from the scriptures that I was in rebellion against a righteous and benevolent God. By His immeasurable grace I found the Bread of Life (Jesus) and He washed my former filthy, perverse, pungent soul with the cleansing and saving blood of God's Lamb; I faithfully and lovingly implore you to call on the Lord Jesus Christ for salvation! Believe and you will receive His forgiveness and eternal life as well as the power to change! Pray:

Father God, I confess, concede, and acknowledge I am a sinner who habitually breaks your laws and I am powerless to consistently obey you! I rightfully deserve the penalty for my sins (death) which is separation from God. I know now that Jesus Christ paid the price with His life for my sins and He has risen from the grave and He is alive forevermore! I reject, renounce, and turn away from my rebellion against you, and from this day forward I will seek to follow your will in this new life that you have granted me! In faith, I thank you for saving me! Amen!

Now you have *eternal* life and enjoy a *favored* and power position with the Father: "He that believeth on the Son hath everlasting life: and he that believeth not the Son shall not see life; but the wrath of God abideth on him" John 3:36. KJV In addition to that permanent position that you possess with God, you have also been accepted into the family of God: "To the praise of the glory of his grace, wherein he hath made us accepted in the beloved" Ephesians 1:6. KJV

And by faith you have secured an inheritance that is incorruptible, imperishable, impeccable, and that will never lose its luster and never be lost. Blessed be the God and Father of our Lord Jesus Christ, which according to his abundant mercy hath begotten us again unto a lively hope by the resurrection of Jesus Christ from the dead, to an inheritance incorruptible, and undefiled, and that fadeth not away, reserved in heaven for you. 1 Peter 1:3-4 KJV

As born-again believers, we should daily bask in the blessed assurance that is ours in this life and the life to come!

Discussion Questions

1) Can you reference a time in your life where you *witnessed*, *walked*, and *worked* in the strength and power of the Lord?

2) What current events or circumstances command you to capture the strength and power of the God of Scripture?

3) What immediate measures must you take in order to experience the strength and power of the God of Scripture?

4) If the God of Scripture is not your personal power source, are you willing to reevaluate and replace your impotent power source with the power of the Almighty?

5) If yes, why? If no, why not?

CHAPTER 2

Identifying the Bully

And the LORD said unto Satan,
Whence comest thou? Then Satan answered the
LORD, and said, From going to and fro in the earth,
and from walking up and down in it.
Job 1:7 KJV

In Greek mythology there is a monstrous hound of hell called Cerberus. He was a hideous and extremely ferocious beast with three heads. As believers and servants of the Lord Jesus Christ, our bully is not a mythical or an imaginary opponent. He is very real, just as rain is very wet! So for our instruction and application, I will characterize and identify this insidious bully as *FWS*. Each letter is analogous to one of the three heads of the dog. The letter *F* represents the *flesh* (sinful and fallen nature of humanity); *W* portrays the *world* (philosophical systems and principles); and *S* sets our sights on our ancient foe who seeks to work us woe (*Satan*). Again, for application let's address the first head of the three-headed dog: the flesh.

Flesh

Beyond skin—the external limiting tissue of our bodies that covers muscles, ligaments, tendons, bones, and countless number of nerves—there is an intangible reality that the Bible calls "the flesh." The Word of God visits and instructs us about the *tangible* (flesh):

"For not all *flesh* is the same, but there is one kind for humans, another for animals, another for birds, and another for fish" (1 Corinthians 15:39 KJV, emphasis added), and the *intangible* (flesh) that denotes mere human nature, the earthly nature of man apart from divine influence, and therefore prone to sin and opposed to God:

[This] I say then, Walk in the Spirit, and ye shall not fulfill the lust of the flesh. Galatians 5:16 KJV

It is the latter definition of the flesh that we will lock our focus on for understanding and practice.

Again, the flesh is situated in the sinful, sensuous, and subversive nature of man. Biblically it denotes the damned nature due to the Adamic curse. It is important to note that we must understand what I refer to as a biblical anthropological assessment of man in order to see ourselves accurately through the lenses of Scripture. The Word of God is our authority that establishes our anthropology as a theology that deals with the origin, nature, and destiny of human beings.

Another term that is synonymous with the term *flesh* is the word *carnal* (*sarx*), which is the same transliteration for the word *flesh*. The Scriptures are clear about the consequences of our carnality.

"For they that are after the flesh do mind the things of the flesh; but they that are after the Spirit the things of the Spirit. For to be carnally minded is death; but to be spiritually minded is life and peace. Because the carnal mind is enmity against God: for it is not subject to the law of God, neither indeed can be. So then they that are in the flesh cannot please God." Romans 8:5-9 KJV

Carnality will never consider the call of concession that Scriptures demands. It will always champion its case of control. And just like its evil twin the *flesh*, it will always lobby its love for leadership. It looks to lead without consideration to its nefarious and noxious nature.

In fact, our flesh is so desperately deep in depravity that it would never subjugate itself to our Lord and God Jesus Christ who transcends all superlatives. Apart from the almighty hand of a merciful and gracious God, we are all destitute and incorrigible.

However, our wretched hearts can be rescued with the hope of heaven. When we ponder the perfect and plentiful promises of God and purchase them by faith, we procure consistent and permanent healing for a heart broken by the horrendous, hideous, and harmful effects of sin.

Park mentally for a period and personalize the following promise from our Father God:

I will seek that which was lost, and bring again that which was driven away and will bind up that which was broken, and will strengthen that which was sick. Ezekiel 34:16a KJV

Too often, like desperate derelicts we drink from the gratuitous goblet that the flesh offers because we are deluded to think that it would provide us with a genuine place of escape, purpose, and peace.

Unfortunately, due to the fact that the flesh is fixed in falsehood, it will always write us a check that we can never cash. It will also severely fall short in supplying the serenity that we are seeking and the present and eternal security that we need. The flesh prides itself as our protector and provider and promises to promote your best interest. However, this so-called assurance is not a *blessed* assurance but a *cursed* assurance that appoints us to a barren wasteland as opposed to the Promised Land.

We must be deliberate in disengaging from the flesh's table of deception and not partake in the flesh's devilish delicacies and denounce its destructive disposition. We must decisively devote ourselves to our divine Creator. God our Father told us that we were made for His pleasure: "Thou art worthy, O Lord, to receive glory and honour power: for thou hast created all things, and for thy pleasure they are and were created" Revelation 4:11. KJV

In order to strengthen our grasp regarding the grip of the flesh, it is critical to consider the objective of the flesh. The flesh encourages us to forfeit the leadership of faith and direction from God and substitute His leadership in our lives with a leadership that is independent of God. Consequently this leads us away from the light and truth and drives us into a direction of darkness and lies. This is why too many of us are parked in a place of spiritual, emotional, and physical challenges that contributes to the chains of oppressive servitude—banking on our biology (body/flesh) will not bolster a better life ! A belief in God that is built and established by God's Word and empowered by His Spirit leads to the abundant life: "I am come that they might have life, and that they might have it more abundantly" John 10:10b KJV.

World

Now let's turn our attention to the second head of the three-headed dog: world.

Love not the world, neither the things that are in the world. If any man love the world, the love of the Father is not in him. 1 John 2:15 KJV

The second head of the three-headed dog is the world's philosophical system attitudes and principles that arrange, order, and govern humanity. It also constitutes the ungodly multitude—the whole mass of men alienated from God, and therefore hostile to the cause of Christ. When our first parents (Adam and Eve) perpetrated treason against our benevolent Creator, the consequence was the corruption and decimation of two domains of man's makeup. Our *conscience*, which gives us the ability to process and conceptualize, and our *affections*, which consist of the things that mean a lot to us and the people we cherish and love.

Because of the fall of man, our conscience and affections became adulterated, which in turn advanced a world that is abounding with principles that promote hardships and ruin. These insidious principles invoke dissension and revoke harmony with our Creator and with our fellow man. In addition, the principles that are consistent with a fallen world are spawned by the satanic influences of *pride, jealousy, rage, prejudice, selfishness, deceit, greed, covetousness, gluttony, violence, and immorality*. This list is not exhaustive, but you get the picture.

Worldly principles promote a world absent of peace but plenteous in pain. Our affections also point us to what we prioritize and devote our lives to. Consequently, too often our hearts are captivated with the concerns of the world: the whole circle of earthly goods, endowments, riches, advantages, pleasures, etc., which although hollow and frail and fleeting, stir desire, seduce us from God, and are obstacles to the cause of Christ.

The world will often manifest itself as a malignant magnet that will even pull professed people of God away from the purpose of God in their lives. In the Word of God, we read about a heartbroken apostle Paul who lost a fellow worker of ministry due to his love for the world: "For

Demas hath forsaken me, having loved this present world, and is departed unto Thessalonica; Crescens to Galatia, Titus unto Dalmatia" 2 Timothy 4:10 KJV.

We are admonished to not adore the world and do not entertain and embrace its advances. Inordinate affection of the world is indicative of a heart that has abandoned his or her Creator. They have also alienated themselves from His perfect and good will for their lives. Consider and capture the truth taught in this passage of Scripture:

For all that is in the world, the lust of the flesh, and the lust of the eyes, and the pride of life, is not of the Father, but is of the world. And the world passeth away, and the lust thereof: but he that doeth the will of God abideth forever. 1 John 2:16-17 KJV

In this passage, we see three prominent positions promoted by the world. First, *the lust of the flesh* is a fixation of feeding the flames of passions that are polluted. For clarity, passion for lovers under the design of God (marital relationship) is pure and precious. It liberates lovers to love lavishly. Passion or lust outside divine lines is licentious and locks lawless lovers in degradation and divine judgment: "Marriage is honorable in all, and the bed undefiled: but whoremongers and adulterers God will judge" Hebrews 13:4 KJV.

Second, *the lust of the eyes* is the consistency of a conscience cemented in covetousness. It is a heart that is abandoned to amassing material possessions, or in many cases, desiring people or things that don't belong to you: "Neither shalt thou desire thy neighbor's wife, neither shalt thou covet thy neighbor's house, his field, or his manservant, or his maidservant, his ox, or his ass, or any [thing] that [is] thy neighbor's" Deuteronomy 5:21 KJV.

Thirdly *the pride of life* is a purposeful and profound preoccupation with power, status, and position of privilege. From the origin of our existence, we witness the world offering a suggestive and attractive proposition of power, position, passion, and privilege to our original parents in the Garden of Eden. Paradise was lost by lust. Eve purged herself from the preoccupation of reverence, loyalty and wonder for God. As a result, she was vulnerable to seduction. Eve yielded to her interest and yoked all mankind to ruin.

As a result, this will demand a Redeemer. Eve was deceived by a duplicitous promise of plans, prospects, pleasure, and purposes independent of God. Sound familiar? It's the same old rap and the same old rascal and the same old result which is, Rebellion and the rupture of our relationship with God.

Now the serpent was more subtle than any beast of the field which the LORD God had made. And he said unto the woman, Yea, hath God said, Ye shall not eat of every tree of the garden? And the woman said unto the serpent, We may eat of the fruit of the trees of the garden: But of the fruit of the tree which is in the midst of the garden, God hath said, Ye shall not eat of it, neither shall ye touch it, lest ye die. And the serpent said unto the woman, Ye shall not surely die: For God doth know that in the day ye eat thereof, then your eyes shall be opened, and ye shall be as gods, knowing good and evil. And when the woman saw that the tree was good for food, and that it was pleasant to the eyes, and a tree to be desired to make one wise, she took of the fruit thereof, and did eat, and gave also unto her husband with her; and he did eat. Genesis 3:1-6 KJV

This leads us to our third head of the bully/dog: Satan.

Satan

Be sober, be vigilant; because your adversary the devil, as a roaring lion,walketh about, seeking whom he may devour: Whom resist stedfast in the faith, knowing that the same afflictions are accomplished in your brethren that are in the world. 1 Peter 5:8-9 KJV

The admonition is forceful—and rightly so—because by nature we have a penchant for arrogance, negligence, and complacency. We embark on a road of error when we entertain an exaggerated estimation of our abilities to defeat Satan. Satan is by far the most cunning and formidable opponent ever to assail men and women made in God's image.

Satan's abhorrence for the Almighty and His anointed is unparalleled. The only love that can exist in his heinous heart is love for himself. There will never be room for anyone else! He is perpetually perverse in his words, thoughts, and deeds. According to the Lord Jesus Christ, he is a murderer and one who lives in lies John 8:44. He is personified by a profound and insatiable contempt for Christ and His church. In comparison to other created beings (demons included), he is a superior satanic sage. It is only by the power of the Holy Spirit that you and I will be able to vanquish his voice and vices. Satan is the undisputed master of manipulation and mayhem.

From the scriptures we can determine that the first man (Adam), wisest and richest man (Solomon), strongest man (Samson), and a man after God's own heart (David) all suffered severe and humiliating losses to Satan. However, the perfect man—the Lord Jesus Christ—thumped that chump at Calvary! This pungent Pariah was no match for the Messiah. The Scripture reminds us that we are overcomers (victors in Christ): "Ye are of God, little children, and have overcome them: because greater is he that is in you, than he that is in the world" 1John 4:4 KJV.

Satan is the prevailing power among the other two heads of this three-headed dog who is the bully. FWS is a terrible tyrant, but he can be consistently trounced through Christ which strengthens us. The Lord that lives in us also leads us to outright obliterate the Devil's power and lies in our lives. Hear and apply what the Lord on high accomplished for you and me:

Forasmuch then as the children are partakers of flesh and blood, he also himself likewise took part of the same; that through death he might destroy him that had the power of death, that is, the devil; And deliver them who through fear of death were all their lifetime subject to bondage. Hebrews 2:14-15 KJV

The book of Ephesians records that our opponent is not human flesh and blood but spiritual (demonic) beings that enjoy influence according to Ephesians 6:12.

For we wrestle not against flesh and blood, but against principalities, against powers, against the rulers of the darkness of this world, against spiritual wickedness in high [places].

But God took on (clothed Himself) in flesh and blood (humanity) in order to deliver a decisive blow to the Devils power and his demons influences in our lives. The Lord's death on the cross brought to pass immediate and absolute deliverance for our souls!!

I really appreciate and make it a practice to apply what the hymn writer Martin Luther recorded:

And though this world, with devils filled should threaten to undo us, we will not fear, for God has willed his truth to triumph through us. The Prince of Darkness grim, we tremble not for him; his rage we can endure, for lo, his doom is sure; one little word shall fell him.[1]

Now that we have identified the bully, let's take our stand against the Bully.

Discussion Questions

1) Why is it an important exercise to identify "the bully"?

2) What is the irony and the truth about the carnal condition?

3) What price do we pay when we buy into and push forward the flesh's promises in our path?

4) What principles and philosophies in your personal life that you promote govern the essential aspects of your life?

5) When you declare someone or something is your adversary, how did you come to that conclusion and is it justifiable and accurate according to the Word of God?

CHAPTER 3

Making a Stand against the Bully

And having done all, to stand.
(Ephesians 6:13c) KJV

Do you remember kindergarten? I sure do! I loved kindergarten. It was an enormously enjoyable and enlightening experience for me personally as a child. The protocol of playing, painting, and a provision of a plate of food and a place mat for nap time. Yes! I was living in paradise! It was indeed a land flowing with milk and cookies.

Consider with me the first four letters in the word *kindergarten*. They spell the word *kind*. When people are kind, their conduct is characterized by a gentleness, benevolence, and gracious disposition. Kindness is an extraordinary virtue, and it espouses love: "Love is patient and kind" (1 Corinthians 13:4b).KJV

To assist us in understanding and adjusting our attitude as they relate to resisting and standing one's ground against a bully, I have elected to employ a lesson from a situation that I was subject to in kindergarten.

My kindergarten experience was endearing and educational. The environment reminded me of a "garden of Kindness" tantamount to the garden of Eden. In our garden of Kindness we learned how to be benevolent beings; however, there was something else I learned in kindergarten. Similar to the garden of Eden, a despot invaded our garden of Kindness and innocence. A belligerent bully was trying to turn my kind garden into a desert of distress!

I remember my opponent well. I will call him RC (regularly cruel). He was unusually big for kindergarten standards. (Giants come in all forms and sizes.) He exhibited knowledge and enjoyed experiences beyond his peers—specifically how to intimidate, utilize intuition to determine who were fearful, and say mean things. He was also very coordinated and athletic for his age. On numerous occasions, this obstinate ogre oppressed me and threatened to treat me to a thumping if I did not give up my cookies. You know, those golden, delicious, buttery, cream-filled cookies that melted in your mouth. I didn't dare denying his demand. It was not my idea to invite a beat down after school. So needless to say, giving up the cookies to RC became a repressive reality for me and a number of my classmates.

One eventful day as the snack time came as usual without delay, I had an incredible thought (because the call of courage was always silenced by "Are you crazy? He will kill you! Give up the cookies!"). But on this day, I thought to myself, *I will not give up my cookies today*, and I did not care what the bully had to say!

Before I knew it, I turned RC away! I took a stand and did not give in to his demand. His face turned into that of a menacing and malicious monster! He made a vow to reward my unexpected insolence. I was invited to a bodacious beat down that I would never forget, which he scheduled for me personally after school.

Now one may ask what manufactured the moxie in me to take a stand against tyranny and move toward liberty. What mitigated my mind of fear? To be honest, it was a passion that purged the terror of the tyrant. I concede that it was not courage. I now understand that it was my penchant to please my palate again with the smooth and sweet, buttery and cream-filled melt-in-your-mouth cookies! Taste transcended my fear. It is important for you to know that my mother at this time had no longer escorted me to school, because to her satisfaction, I had demonstrated the discipline to stay on the path going home so her company was no longer necessary.

Can you believe that there was a time in our country that children could walk home or play without getting abducted and assaulted by an adult? Forgive me for my digression. Times have really changed! So after innumerable walks, I was very familiar with my pathway to home.

This would prove to be very beneficial for my bout with the bully. Unknown to my adversary, I had strategically concealed an equalizer (a sturdy and solid stick) on the way before school that day. To this day, I cannot tell you why. It's possible that I had entertained standing up to the bully in my head. As a child, I was not deficient in imagination. So it's plausible that I processed in my mind whipping that bully a hundred times.

When RC saw me after school, I took flight! He began his hot pursuit, as well as a group of spectators. As he was closing ground, I just happened to be at the precise location of my concealed equalizer. I guess RC underestimated the passion and now courage of a young boy and his loyalty to his creamy, buttery cookies. And with the element of surprise, I overcame my opponent and I did not ever yield my cookies to the bully again.

We have a much more lethal weapon to strike into the heart and cut off the heads of the bully: the Word of God! For the Word of God is quick and powerful and sharper than any two-edged sword (Hebrews 4:12a).

In order to make a stand against the bully (FWS), we must be cognizant of his devices or he will dupe us into a thought life of destruction. In addition, we must be familiar and study the scouting report on our opponent: the Bible. When I was a collegiate student athlete (football), we would extensively prepare for the upcoming opponent physically and mentally. Physical preparation consisted of one-on-one and team drills designed to simulate playing or game-day conditions. A demonstration of the opponent's offensive and defensive plays and formations were assigned by the demonstration or (Demo) team. Preparation for the week's opponent was also supplemented with cardio (wind sprints) and weight training.

The mental aspect involved hours of film work. An examination and study of the opponents' offensive and defensive plays and formations were placed on a whiteboard, and a scouting report that consisted of the opponent personnel, plays, formations, special teams, as well as their strengths and weaknesses and tendencies was scrutinized. We also had to be astute in our awareness with respect to our team's weaknesses and vulnerabilities because a very capable and worthy opponent would naturally exploit them for its advantage. The time usually invested for preparation was typically from thirty-five to forty hours a week.

Likewise, it is absolutely imperative that we commit ourselves to a deliberate exercise of intense and focused study of God's scouting report—the Word of God—so that we may prevent FWS from having his way with us. For instance, from studying God's scouting report— which by the way is the most impeccable and infinite source of information the world has ever known—there are a number of strategies that FWS will seek to seduce us with. I would point you to five that would prove to be effective in rendering FWS ineffective in efforts to take you out:

Invoke our instincts
Intensify his influence
Invigorate our intemperance
Incite intimidation
Instigate our insurgence

Invoking Our Instincts

FWS (flesh, world, Satan) pleads and calls us to usurp the Lord's leadership of the Spirit and promote our natural instincts as our authority. FWS encourages us to promote and establish our instincts as our reference for all answers. This capricious coward calls us to trust our instincts and not God. But the scouting report (the Holy Scriptures) states that our instincts are unreliable and extremely dishonest and debased—steeped in seduction and instability. This is why our Father insists that we trust Him and not rely on a rebellious heart.

Trust in the LORD with all thine heart; and lean not unto thine own understanding. In all thy ways acknowledge him, and he shall direct thy paths. Proverbs 3:5-6 KJV

For I know that in me (that is, in my flesh,) dwelleth no good thing: for to will is present with me; but [how] to perform that which is good I find not. Romans 7:18 KJV

It is clear from Scripture that our natural and innate instincts insidiously lead us to a path paved with perverse proclivities that lead to compromise, costly decisions, and a catastrophic conclusion:"

There is a way which seemeth right unto a man, but the end thereof [are] the ways of death. Proverbs 14:12 KJV

Oftentimes our instincts will incline us to take flight from embracing any responsibility for displaying rebellion against our Father. For instance, when our first original parents Adam and Eve transgressed against God, their instincts induced them to cover themselves in fig leaves and to run and hide themselves away from God as opposed to running to God in humility to take ownership for what they had done.

"And when the woman saw that the tree [was] good for food, and that it [was] pleasant to the eyes, and a tree to be desired to make [one] wise, she took of the fruit thereof, and did eat, and gave also unto her husband with her; and he did eat.

And the eyes of them both were opened, and they knew that they [were] naked; and they sewed fig leaves together, and made themselves aprons. And they heard the voice of the LORD God walking in the garden in the cool of the day: and Adam and his wife hid themselves from the presence of the LORD God amongst the trees of the garden" Genesis 3:6-8 KJV

When the United States economy is upside down and depressed too often, instincts are not denied, and consequently they dictate the direction of people's behavior with respect of giving. Generosity and sharing will take a backseat to self-centeredness.

When there is impeccable evidence that an individual violated a law his instincts will lead him to lie, blame or not take personal responsibility. Instincts are usually impulsive and are indicative of the weakness of our humanity as well as the depravity that is deep in our hearts. FWS invokes our instincts for the purpose of mastering our lives.

Intensify His Influence

Influence is defined as "the power to effect decisions." The three-headed dog powerfully exerts his evil influence enslaving and eviscerating the hearts of man, and encouraging envy, strife, mayhem, and destruction on the pillars that make up a sound society: family, government and church. FWS is satanically suspending our society in lawlessness and wickedness: "We know that we are of God, and the whole world lieth in wickedness" 1 John 5:19.KJV

Galatians chapter five expresses a cogent and clear characterization of one of the heads of FWS (flesh) that influences our lives and invites dire consequences:

Now the works of the flesh are manifest, which are [these]; Adultery, fornication, uncleanness, lasciviousness, Idolatry, witchcraft, hatred, variance, emulations, wrath, strife, seditions, heresies, Envyings, murders, drunkenness, revellings, and such like: of the which I tell you before, as I have also told [you] in time past, that they which do such things shall not inherit the kingdom of God. Galatians 5:19-21 KJV

The most lethal and most effective power that we have to not just neutralize but decimate the bully influence in our lives is the Holy Spirit and His Word!

For though we walk in the flesh, we do not war after the flesh: For the weapons of our warfare are not carnal, but mighty through God to the pulling down of strong holds; Casting down imaginations, and every high thing that exalteth itself against the knowledge of God, and bringing into captivity every thought to the obedience of Christ. 2 Corinthians 10:4-5 KJV

Invigorating Our Intemperance

The third strategy that the bully will try to employ is to invigorate our intemperance. In other words, he will energize our lack of self-control in various aspects of our lives, especially in the arena of appetites, affections, activities, and attitude. To illustrate, an undisciplined mouth will bring misfortune. Also a deficiency of discipline in what we entertain and embrace encourages error and an inescapable judgment. If one cannot master his attitude and emotions, it is inevitable that he or she will be vulnerable to the bully's aversive advances! He that hath no rule over his own spirit is like a city that is broken down, and without walls. Proverbs 25:28 KJV

We live in an impetuous culture. There is little or zero consideration of consequences for lawlessness. The following statements epitomize the depth of what I refer to as the delusional descent of intemperance:

All the things I really like to do are either illegal, immoral, or fattening. Alexander Woollcott[1]

I seek the utmost pleasure and the least pain.—Plautus[2]

The scouting report (God's Word) mandates a mortification of our fleshly passions in order to maintain a majestic position with God: "And they that are Christ's have crucified the flesh with the affections and lusts" Galatians 5:24 KJV.

Incite Intimidation

Intimidation intoxicates FWS. He knows that intimidation ensures his chance of successfully dominating your life. He leads you by your nose with a hideous hook! Fear is situated in the weakness of our humanity and holds countless numbers of people hostage. But the power to overcome fear is not innate or developed by natural causes or conditioning. Our scouting report reveals that "God hath not given us the spirit of fear; but of power, and of love, and of a sound mind" (2 Timothy 1:7). "There is no fear in love; but perfect love casteth out fear: because fear hath torment" 1 John 4:18a.KJV

The only way that Satan gets into your head to intimidate you is by way of an invitation that you give him. When we entertain his lies and embrace them as fact, we fold to his treachery! We must stop leasing space in our minds to this loser and level him with the truth. Here is a passage of Scripture that rips the hinges and destroys the doors of FWS intimidation:

And what is the exceeding greatness of his power to us-ward who believe, according to the working of his mighty power, Which he wrought in Christ, when he raised him from the dead, and set him at his own right hand in the heavenly places, Far above all principality, and power, and might, and dominion, and every name that is named, not only in this world, but also in that which is to come. Ephesians 1:19-21 KJV

Have you ever given serious thought to how much power it takes to resurrect a person back from the grave after he has been dead for four days? When you and I can internally exercise this phenomenal truth in our lives, we will rout and render the bully's lies utterly useless. This truth will tear you away from trepidation and transport you to a tall and triumphant platform. To recapture the territory that has been ripped from his control, the bully will make a desperate call to the rebellion and hostility that is in the heart by nature. He wants to instigate your insurgence.

Instigating Your Insurgence

For to be carnally minded is death; but to be spiritually minded is life and peace. Because the carnal mind is enmity against God: for it is not subject to the law of God, neither indeed can be. Romans 8:6-7 KJV

Because we have a disposition directed by depravity, the bully will try to take advantage of the natural hostility that all humans have because of the fall of man. It's inconceivable to consider that there is a part of us that champions anarchy in our hearts and aligns itself with the archenemy of God and man. Again I submit to you that we do not have to concede to the cry of the carnality in our hearts because power of the cross of Christ delivered a crushing blow and buried that old body of death in Christ! Henceforth, we walk in newness of life!

Know ye not, that so many of us as were baptized into Jesus Christ were baptized into his death? Therefore we are buried with him by baptism into death: that like as Christ was raised up from the dead by the glory of the Father, even so we also should walk in newness of life. Romans 6:3-4 KJV

We do not have to relinquish this reality of hope! Remember, greater is the Lord's presence in our hearts than the external and internal pressure from FWS.

Discussion Questions

1) What are the factors and motivation that moves individuals to take a stand against an oppressor?
2) Currently is there any person, thing, or situation that you must take a stand against?
3) Has there ever been an instance in your life where a desire or appetite moved you to do the unexpected?

4) How can faith, knowledge, and implementation of the Holy Scriptures aid you in standing up and defeating the bully in your life?

5) How will knowledge of the five strategies of the bully be beneficial to you as you stand up to the bully in your life?

CHAPTER 4

The Arrogance of Self-Autonomy

Apart from me you can do nothing.
John 15:5c KJV

One of the core beliefs of secular humanists is that by science and reason, they conclude that their existence is independent from any divine creator. Consequently, they conclude that they are the center and catalyst for civilization. Consider the following excerpt that is taken from their manifesto:

Humanism is a democratic and ethical life stance, which affirms that human beings have the right and responsibility to give meaning and shape to their own lives. It stands for the building of a more humane society through an ethic based on human and other natural values in the spirit of reason and free inquiry through human capabilities. It is not theistic, and it does not accept supernatural views of reality. International Humanist and Ethical Union[1]

I submit to you that this secular and humanistic declaration is an audacious absorption of abject arrogance and self-autonomy.

Creating a hostile environment (in our minds and heart) for the purposes of reclaiming and maintaining personal victory must start with this absolute admission: apart from the Lord Jesus Christ, you will not successfully accomplish anything. In the economy of God, independence of God is not only deceitful and delusional but it will also leave you directionless. We need the Good Shepherd in our lives! "All we like sheep have gone astray; we have turned everyone to his own way" Isaiah 53:6a KJV.

When we are independent of God's leadership, we poison all streams of relationships—personally, professionally, and publicly. We don't heal; we will continue to hurt others and ourselves. Leadership apart from the Lord is always a losing proposition. When the Lord emphatically stated, "Apart from me you can do nothing," *nothing* means *nothing.* Your prospect of success will be tossed in the sea of obscurity without the Captain of all souls at the helm of your life.

There will be no sound or substantive relationships, proper perspectives and purposes, strength and stability, peace and prosperity. You will not receive accurate advice and answers, victory from vices, protection and power, nor sanctification, satisfaction for the soul and holiness that comes from the heart of God without the Lord's leadership. It is essential that He enjoys the role of Shepherd for our lives! The Word of God reminds us that when the Lord is our Shepherd, we shall not be deposited into deficiency: "The LORD is my shepherd; I shall not want" Psalm 23:1 KJV.

However, the arrogance of self-autonomy will always be associated and identified with a bad shepherd as opposed to the Good Shepherd (the Lord Jesus Christ). You will always be in a deplorable degree of deficiency. Furthermore, when we try to lead our lives without the Lord, it will drive us away to languish in a labyrinth of limbo.

Abandon the advice of arrogance and sever yourself from self-autonomy. Exterminate the exercise of ego (edging God out). Look to the Lord and *He* will lead to streams that will refresh your heart and renew your soul. He is the true and genuine guiding Light that will lead and keep you on His path and not your own:

Hear what the Lord Jesus Christ said about himself in the gospel of John; Then spake Jesus again unto them, saying, I am the light of the world: he that followeth me shall not walk in darkness, but shall have the light of life. John 8:12 KJV

Finally, there is a considerable degree of conceit in a conscience captured by arrogance and self-autonomy.

Time is not subject to man. Time does not stop for man. Time cannot be bribed or negotiated with. But time is subjected to the one who has no beginning or end, and it must follow His orders: "I am the Alpha and the Omega," says the Lord God, "who is, and who was, and who is to come, the Almighty" Revelation 1:8 KJV.

Time has its way with the arrogant just as a tsunami has its way with villages built with mud and straw! But the master of time not only will silence a raging sea but will cause time to stand still.

The arrogance of self-autonomy abrogates the truth regarding the immeasurable distance between Creator God and diminutive man. The Apostle Paul clearly conveys this truth in the following passage.

Oh, the depth of the riches of the wisdom and knowledge of God! How unsearchable his judgments, and his paths beyond tracing out! Romans 11:33 KJV

It's important to note that this appalling attitude of arrogance owes its origin not to a terrestrial being but to the heart of a celestial being. It is his spirit that is the influence behind all arrogance and self-exaltation.

How you have fallen from heaven, O morning star, son of the dawn! You have been cast down to the earth, you who once laid low the nations! You said in your heart, "I will ascend to heaven; I will raise my throne above the stars of God; I will sit enthroned on the mount of assembly, on the utmost heights of the sacred mountain. I will ascend above the tops of the clouds; I will make myself like the Most High." Isaiah 14:12-14 KJV

For application I ascribe Lucifer's five *I wills* as the "five mental ills." I believe they epitomize the arrogance of self-autonomy that is a life independent of God. It is the height of self-deification.

God hates the proud but gives grace to the humble:
But he giveth more grace. Wherefore he saith, God resisteth the proud, but giveth grace unto the humble. Submit yourselves therefore to God. Resist the devil, and he will flee from you. James 4:6-7 KJV

I would like to leave you with a closing thought:
I believe that in the sight of God Arrogance is an offensive display that suggests you are superior in every way. But not too far away adversity is on its way, to remind you that you are only a piece of clay, and the LORD OF LORDS WILL HAVE HIS WAY! Pastor Bernard King Sr.

Discussion Questions

1) How do individuals defend a life absent from the Almighty?
2) What kinds of impact of a life without lordship have on the most salient aspects of your life (private, personal, professional, and public)?

3) If you are arrested by arrogance, what steps should one take in order to be liberated from the lies of arrogance?

4) As you examine your past and present life, did you ever edge God out, and what did you learn from that experience?

5) What are the people, things, and situations that will cause you to be vulnerable to self-autonomy?

CHAPTER 5

Meet My Friend: MR. MAP

O how love I thy law! it is my meditation all the day.
(Psalm 119:97 KJV)

When my three sons were young children, I wanted them to have a sincere interest in the Word of God. I wanted them to know that life doesn't consist of an incessant investment of indulgence. Considered what the Lord Jesus said: "Man shall not live by bread alone but every word that proceedeth out of the mouth of God" Matthew 4:4b. KJV

At this season in their life, I wanted to take advantage of their minds and hearts while they were still pliable and soft—which, by the way, are the perfect conditions for the Spirit of God to work. When the head and heart are hard like dried cement, it's difficult to repent.

So in order to assist my sons in comprehending and internalizing the importance of the Holy Scriptures in their hearts and minds, God graciously gave me a tool to teach them the discipline of developing a relationship with God according to the Scriptures. That tool and tutor is "MR. MAP." Each letter in the term *MR. MAP* reflects five disciplines that will direct and develop a dedicated disciple of the Lord. MR. MAP represents a righteous man who is faithful to partner with you in practical ways that point you to the purposes and the power of God's Word in your life.

M = memorization
R = reading
M = meditation
A = application
P = prayer

Being physically fit does not happen by osmosis. It is a reward from being obedient to an order of disciplines (exercises). Additionally, you need a personal trainer or authority who is proficiently knowledgeable and rich in experience! Likewise, being spiritually fit demands a devotee (you) and a divine trainer so we can run His race and position ourselves consistently on the victors' platform than in the ditch of defeat.

Unfortunately, in the body of Christ, disciplined members (disciples) are the exception to the rule. Make it a point not to be a disciple who is deliberately deficient in discipline.

In order to create a hostile environment for personal victory and to reclaim and maintain that victory, we must be disciplined. Our Father has called us to excellence, and He will give a reward. Consider what the absolutely infallible and reliable text records with respect to discipline:

And whatsoever ye do, do it heartily, as to the Lord, and not unto men; Knowing that of the Lord ye shall receive the reward of the inheritance: for ye serve the Lord Christ. Colossians 3:24 KJV

Aristotle once said, "We are what we repeatedly do: Excellence then is not an act but a habit."[1]

If we are honest, a good number of us are not in a good place with our spiritual fitness. We have been resting in the reclining chair of complacency, apathy, indifference, and in some cases, ignorance. We are getting obese from greasy grace and consequently slipping into a carnal coma!

And that, knowing the time, that now [it is] high time to awake out of sleep: for now [is] our salvation nearer than when we believed. Romans 13:11 KJV

Let's stop sitting on a couch that is in compliance with our carnal nature. Toss the potato chip bag of past accomplishments and disappointments. As servants of God, we either strive for the excellence that is for His glory or we are stagnant and smell as opposed to being a sweet aroma to our Lord.

MR. MAP comes alongside to assist your attention and application and appreciation for the Scriptures. Let's start with the first discipline.

Meditation

This book of the law shall not depart out of thy mouth; but thou shalt *meditate* therein day and night, that thou mayest observe to do according to all that is written therein: for then thou shalt make thy way prosperous, and then thou shalt have good success. Joshua 1:8 KJV, emphasis added

A new leader had been appointed for a nation under God Almighty! His predecessor (Moses) primed him with some salient advice that would make the change in leadership a smooth transition and leave the nation with a leader who was led by the Lord. Moses understood that you can't lead the people to God if you are not familiar with God. How can a man know how God thinks, if he does not think with His Word? We know that what we think can influence our behavior: "For as he thinketh in his heart, so is he" Proverbs 23:7b KJV.

Therefore Moses charged Joshua that he must meditate in order to maximize optimal success in his new appointment! Likewise, we must purpose to practice the first discipline of MR. MAP (mediation), which will lead to establishing a hostile environment for FWS.

The object of meditation for a disciple of Christ is always His infallible and inspired Word. We read the Word with purpose and thoughtfulness; we mentally park on the principles for the purpose of application and understanding. Furthermore, the Author of the Scriptures aligns our mind and our conclusions with His mind.

Contemplation is captured and driven by concentration on the Scriptures and not on one's breathing or an incessant repetition of mantras. Thinking is not eliminated but engaged. This is the type of meditation that is authorized and sanctioned by the true God and eternal life Jesus Christ. Any other form of spiritual contemplation is absolutely prohibited according to the Scriptures. Meditation motivated and mastered under mysticism is forbidden for all true followers of God. The Scripture powerfully pounds the point that we are to meditate on the Word of God.

But his delight is in the law of the LORD; and in his law doth he *meditate* day and night. Psalm 1:2 KJV, emphasis added

I will meditate in thy precepts, and have respect unto thy ways. Psalms 119:15 KJV

When we meditate, we ponder on the what, why, and the how of the text. We visit things like, Who is speaking? and What is the context of the text? and What is the verse saying or not saying? and Is there a personal instruction for me or for others? and Is there an admonition or a promise? Again, this is the kind of meditation that is encouraged and sanctioned by Scripture.

When the faculty of the mind is fixed in a biblical framework, it will forward success in all facets of our lives (Joshua 1:8). Meditating on the Word of God will place you in a position to surpass those who have instructed you in the things of God: "I have more understanding than all my teachers: for thy testimonies are my meditation" Psalm 119:99 KJV.

To assist my appropriation of this truth, I asked a personal friend of mine who is a very reputable and accomplished professional chef about the benefit of marinating meat in preparation for a meal.

He shared with me that whenever you marinate meat, you are altering the chemistry of the meat. The acidity of the marinade restructures the texture by tenderizing and permeating the protein (flesh) with flavor.

Prior to my discussion with my chef friend, God gave me the word marinate when I was pondering the practice and discipline of meditation. Thus, after my lesson in cooking preparation for a succulent and savory steak, I was able to arrive at an application.

The mind represents the meat and the marinade (or solution) that will restructure my thought life is the Scriptures. And remember, how we think gives tremendous weight to our conduct. The psalmist petitioned, "Order my steps in thy word: and let not any iniquity have dominion over me" (Psalm 119:133 KJV). Meditation is a discipline that will dictate your direction. It will also promote proactive steps that will prevent the influence of FWS in your decisions.

Reading

The second discipline of MR. MAP is *reading*. For a disciple of the Lord Jesus Christ, reading is indeed fundamental. It is also a recommended mandate from the Word of God. The Lord God even expects those who enjoy leadership to make it their practice to read the Word of God.

And it shall be with him, and he shall *read* therein all the days of his life: that he may learn to fear the LORD his God, to keep all the words of this law and these statutes, to do them. Deuteronomy 17:19 KJV

Nehemiah read and engaged in expository teaching of the Word of God: "So they read in the book in the law of God distinctly, and gave the sense, and caused [them] to understand the reading" Nehemiah 8:8 KJV.

And the apostle Paul communicated a charge to church leadership with respect to the nonnegotiable discipline of reading the Scriptures in church: "Till I come, give attendance to reading, to exhortation, to doctrine" 1 Timothy 4:13 KJV.

My friends, reading will reward you immensely and you will discover a vast vault of truth and wisdom that is inexhaustible! Reading the Word of God represents a reverence for God, a revival and restoration for the thirsty and empty soul. It realigns my thought life and reminds me what is really important. The skill set to read is essential to thrive and be successful in this life as well as the next life.

I remember the first time that I was going to embark on my first long-distance trip by car. Prior to this adventure, the greatest amount of driving time that I had endured was an hour and a half tops. So I purpose to engage on an twenty hour trip on I-95. I will always remember the words of encouragement from my dad. He said, "If you can read and pay attention and obey the signs, you will not get lost."

This was well before GPS. And you know what? He was right. Have you ever entertained the thought that most people are misplaced and lost because they do not read the Word of God? They are lost in their marital relationships, parenting their children, singleness, social and professional life, and even in their religious and spiritual practices. Remember, His word is a lamp unto our feet and a light unto our path Psalm 119:105.

Memorization

Memorization is an essential discipline to help you stay intimate with the Master. It is a lethal weapon against the lies of FWS.

It provides an excellent defense plan that will defeat the schemes of your own deceitful heart. Hear and embrace the exhortation of the Word of God with respect to keeping a consistent path that characterizes Christlikeness:

Wherewithal shall a young man cleanse his way? by taking heed thereto according to thy word. With my whole heart have I sought thee: O let me not wander from thy commandments. Thy *word have I hid in mine heart*, that I might not sin against thee. Psalm 119:9-11 KJV, emphasis added)

The Word of God is a priceless treasure that must be deeply, discreetly kept in a secure place: "More to be desired are they than gold, yea, than much fine gold: sweeter also than honey and the honeycomb" (Psalm 19:10 KJV).

This practice is paramount for personal victory in your life. To assist us in our application, I have employed the example of an ATM. We utilize the ATM for money transactions. In order for you to secure monies from your bank account, you insert your bank card. Then you give the appropriate access code and decide the source (checking or savings) to get your money. After you have secured your money, the ATM provides a receipt. When you are in need, you do not want to read "insufficient funds" on your receipt. You can avoid that dilemma by consistently depositing money and being conscientious of your balance in the bank.

When we are in need of spiritual resources, it is essential to know that you have a substantial amount of "money" (the Word of God) in your heart. I promise you that there will be a time where you will need to make a withdrawal from your spiritual bank! Your faith account must be full!

Let the word of Christ dwell in you richly in all wisdom. Colossians 3:16a KJV

The Word of God not only should be deposited in your heart and soul, but it should also be thriving and growing.

Application

Application is indicative of the authority of the Word of God in one's life. The power of God is experienced when we practice the principles.

Application coincides with being a law-abiding citizen. Consider: if we do not apply the traffic laws, we invite penalties and consequences. We will also create and contribute to a world of chaos and crisis.

One of the main obstructions to application of the Word of God is our obstinate disposition. When we are adamant in our indifference, we only apply what we qualify. One must realize that such a practice dismisses the divine authority in one's life. Too many people who are occupying the church are only hearers and not doers. This places right up front the futility of hearing and reading without application. Hear what the scriptures have to say about being all ears and no personal execution of instruction.

But be ye doers of the word, and not hearers only, deceiving your own selves. For if any be a hearer of the word, and not a doer, he is like unto a man beholding his natural face in a glass: For he beholdeth himself, and goeth his way, and straightway forgetteth what manner of man he was. James 1:22-24 KJV

Early in my walk with the Lord, my loving, but faithful and firm, heavenly Father attended to my need in this area of application—specifically with forgiveness. The Lord Jesus taught us the mandate of forgiveness. Supernaturally it is a part of our spiritual DNA:

For if ye forgive men their trespasses, your heavenly Father will also forgive you: But if ye forgive not men their trespasses, neither will your Father forgive your trespasses. Matthew 6:14-15 KJV

As a newborn in Christ, life had meaning and color. Absolute truth was a reality, and love was very real. I was basking in my newfound relationship that by faith I knew would forever eclipse all others for eternity. While I was entertaining in my heart and mind the magnitude of forgiveness that was wonderfully mine, floating on the ocean of His forgiveness and mercy, I could hear the words of my Lord say, *Did you forgive your father?*

"Oh, Lord, You know that I forgave my father when I received your forgiveness' for my sins and made you Lord of my life!

By his Spirit I heard, *"Not Matthew, your stepfather, but your biological father, Ray. I want you to forgive him just as I have forgiven you."*

My recollection about my biological father was that he was not a good man and that he abdicated his role in my life when I was very young. And my faithful and true Lord wanted to deliver me from the deep-seated resentment and unforgiving spirit that was cemented in my conscience and harbored in my heart toward my biological father.

My reaction to my Lord's instruction was unfortunately objectionable and overflowing with a river of rage. I resented the fact that my heavenly Father would tell me to do such a thing! I judged Him to be exceptionally wrong on this directive, and I begin to excoriate His expectation of me. After a spell of spewing the foul and sickening sewage that was in my heart, the following statement from my Lord eviscerated my soul: *You said that you love Me more than anyone and anything.* Now we know that the Word of God states:

Faithful [are] the wounds of a friend; but the kisses of an enemy [are] deceitful. Proverbs 27:6 KJV

The words that I received which I believed came from the Holy spirit struck my soul like a sharp two edged sword of truth was thrust deeply in my hardened heart. I personally experienced the wounding of my faithful Lord and friend Jesus Christ!

My Lord was calling me out on the application of forgiveness! Instead of reading and hearing "forgive one another just as Christ has forgiven you," I had to die (to self) in order to apply! I am a witness about the power of application for liberation for the soul. Too many of you are incarcerated by an insidious and indignant attitude of unforgiveness. Your belligerent ball and chains of bitterness and contempt continues to cauterize your conscience. Obey and apply, and you will immediately fly to victory! Again application is attached to the authority in your life.

Prayer

It's only appropriate to close our fifth and final discipline with prayer. The discipline of prayer is a dynamic doorway to the divine. The Scriptures call us to pray always and do not falter.

One of the weapons that our bully FWS wields and uses to war against us is our humanity. Sometimes our humanity is tantamount to a heavy handed heavyweight landing a wicked haymaker to our head. He wants to knock us into tomorrow in the area of prayer. A lack of prayer communicates a compromise of power and communion with Christ. It is a sign of carelessness. It cultivates callousness towards the concerns of God and His Spirit.

The call of compromise will sound like "sweet nothings" to your ear. My friends don't be deceived. Don't listen to the Devil. The gospel group the Winans served us an inspirational and compelling piece about prayer. In their song "Don't Be Deceived," one of the verses states, "God says to pray, you should pray always and never faint. But the Devil says it's fine to pray when their time, and you say OK. "Don't you be deceived."[2]

Here is what the Word of God says: "Pray without ceasing" (1 Thessalonians 5:17 KJV).

When our Lord was hours away from the cross, he was subjected to extreme anguish and distress. The prospects of embracing our evil hearts of sin and depravity (and thereby causing immediate separation from His Father) buffeted Him mercilessly. He prevailed with the power of prayer! However His closest disciples where overwhelmed by the fury of their flesh and failed their master when He needed them the most. The Lord, under the onslaught of grief and despair, asked them to watch and pray with Him! But again they were crushed under the weight of their carnality and fell asleep!

Jesus admonished Peter by saying to him, "Watch and *pray*, that ye enter not into temptation: the spirit indeed is willing, but the flesh is weak" (Matthew 26:41 KJV, emphasis added). Basically, be on the alert and pray! This will keep you from succumbing to the pressure cooker of carnality.

The Lord Jesus Christ completely characterizes our approach toward agonizing and anxiety-filled situations. He did not have what many pastors and people of faith have: a "P and P issue." That is, one's presentation is incongruent with his practice. Occupied in an oppressed state and tremendously taxed, tortured, with a devastating barrage of distress, He positioned Himself in the power of prayer and persevered! Three times He prayed, "Not my will but your will be done." The application that we should adopt for the purpose of reclaiming and maintaining personal victory is, "I will not cancel the cup that You have called me to drink." Remember, the call of carnality will always champion capitulation to self.

Carnality seeks to condition your conscience to close the door to the spirit of God's influence. We must always pray—and then pray some more. To reinforce our resolve to pray, consider the following tool that will encourage and escalate your prayer life. To PRAY means:

Position ourselves in His power
Respectfully requesting with resolve
Approaching His throne in faith
Yoke and yield ourselves to His will in humility

Without prayer, you have no intimacy and power to maintain and reclaim personal victory. When you read the Word of God, remember to invite MR. MAP along. He will assist you in opening your eyes to see the wonder and power of the Word of God in your life.

Discussion Questions

1) Why is it essential to exercise a biblical form of meditation?

2) What are the implications of a disciplined spiritual life in Christ?

3) How do you know when you are deficient in spiritual fitness?

4) When do you come to the realization that you are spiritually fit?

5) Why do so many professing believers possess a plethora of knowledge but are poor in the application of that knowledge in their spiritual life?

CHAPTER 6

A Man or Women under Authority

For I am a man under authority, having soldiers under
me: and I say to this man, Go, and he goeth; and to
another, Come, and he cometh; and to my servant,
Do this, and he doeth it.
(Matthew 8:9 KJV)

This passage points to the profound and impressive faith of a Roman military leader. He is clear and coherent and enjoys a substantial command of his authority and his limitations as a commander. He absolutely understood that the Lord Jesus Christ enjoys all power and authority! His testimony of trust and his exercise of extraordinary faith even excited our Lord: "When Jesus heard it, he marvelled, and said to them that followed, Verily I say unto you, I have not found so great faith, no, not in Israel" Matthew 8:10 KJV.

To experience and exercise the skill set necessary for creating a hostile environment for the flesh, and to reclaim and maintain personal victory, it's vital that we feature a faith that reveals the facts that the Lord is the authority of our lives. Our flesh features a faith that reveals a fixation with self-autonomy and insubordination to our supreme Lord and God. Our good and gracious God expects us to assume the position of absolute and willing subordination to Him. We must willingly elevate the King of Kings and the Lord of Lords. For those who occupy an overtly obstinate stance, the King will obliterate your pride and pummel you to a place of unmitigated veneration: "For it is written, [As] I live, saith the Lord, every knee shall bow to me, and every tongue shall confess to God" (Romans 14:11 KJV).

Authority means the power or right to give orders, make decisions, and enforce obedience. This Roman military leader applied a faith that fixed him in the fact that just as his superiors could give him direct orders and he could also give orders to those who were under his authority, he concluded that the Lord Jesus Christ's authority exceeded any jurisdiction and was not even challenged or limited or bounded to any laws on earth. There was no doubt that the Lord Jesus could give the direct command and the sickness that grievously afflicted his servant would be immediately removed. Permit me to shed some context. This will assist us in capturing the lesson and augmenting our application.

The man that the Lord Jesus Christ recognized as having an impressive faith is an officer (centurion) in the Roman army, which means he had one hundred men under his authority. He was also a Gentile. Gentiles were prohibited from being invited to Jewish homes. The Jewish people generally despised and loathed the Roman soldiers. Rome had occupied their land and ruled with a heavy hand.

However, the Roman officer exhibited the character and faith that is worthy of attention. His faith carried him over the walls of status and segregation. He made a deliberate decision to not be deterred by social and religious obstacles on the behalf of his slave. This was noteworthy because slaves did not enjoy personal rights. They were considered as mere property and were always subject to their masters' prerogative. If a slave was stricken with sickness and due to that sickness no longer able to meet his or her master's expectations, the slave owner could discard and replace the unhealthy slave or even put him to death.

The centurion contradicted cultural norms and customs. He cared for his slave. His heart reflected a huge degree of humility and hope. Without any hesitation, he said, "Lord, just give the command, and my servant will be healed."

Just like that centurion, our faith should be in overdrive and override any obstacles that prevent us from experiencing personal victory. We live and experience personal defeat and penalize ourselves with self-imposed inordinate obsessions and obstructions of liberty. This is oftentimes associated with our objection to the Lord's authority— specifically His Scriptures and His Spirit in our lives. This invites a personal inquiry: Who is the consistent authority in your life?

Your honest answer will give you a specific revelation with respect to your position of liberty and victory in your walk with God. When we habitually submit to God as our authority, we have everything we need in order to realize victory over any vice—fear, gluttony, anger, bigotry, immorality, gambling, drugs, and drunkenness. The aforementioned list is not exhaustive; however, you can add to the list any life-dominating influence that is exacting the authority in your life. The Lord Jesus Christ reserves the utmost exclusive right to reign in your life. If He is not on the throne of your thoughts and heart as oppose to your personal feelings; then you must make a deliberate decision to remove and dethrone the deceitful dictator. There must be a new government establish by the Holy Spirit. We will visit the leadership of the Holy Spirit in the next chapter.

As disciples, we must move from the "feeling station" and fill up at the "faith station." Faith is essential, and it is also a mandate to move yourself by His grace under His authority:

But without faith, it is impossible to please him: for he that cometh to God must believe that he is, and that he is a rewarder of them that diligently seek him. (Hebrews 11:6 KJV)

Consider your current commander in your life. Who is calling all the shots? Place him under the superior scrutiny of Scripture. Examine that authority with the following questions: Can your authority command death to release his captive? Can he command the demons to surrender their possession of a soul and depart and never return? Can he defy gravity and nature and charge a sea to cease its roaring?

Can he totally decimate a fortified spiritual or fleshly stronghold in your mind and heart? Has he decreed eternal destruction and damnation to the Devil and his demons? Is he the undisputed supreme and absolute Savior for all? If you can't answer unequivocally in the affirmative to each and every question, revoke and reject that treacherous monarch! Replace him with the wonderful master of miracles, mighty God, matchless in love and mercy, magnanimous in forgiveness! Magnificent in magnitude is the Lord Jesus Christ. He is the true God and eternal life.

Discussion Questions

1) How do you identify and certify the authority in your life?
2) When and how do you replace the Lord's authority over your life?
3) What kind of faith impresses the Lord?
4) Can you identify and list a number of unlawful authorities that you have submitted to in the past and are possibly currently submitting to?
5) Why is it essential to consistently examine the authority that you submit to?

CHAPTER 7

The Leadership of the Holy Spirit

For as many as are led by the Spirit of God,
they are the sons of God.
(Romans 8:14 KJV)

Today's idolatrous indoctrination of video and computer games and Internet social networking venues like MySpace, Facebook, and now Twitter has undoubtedly unfolded a generation disconnected from reality and has also delivered an epidemic of unfit and unhealthy kids and young adults. For the most part, electronic entertainment is usually not coupled with accountability or policed by responsibility.

Two salient standards of scrutiny that should be implemented with computer and video games are *measured monitoring* (with spiritual wisdom and biblical guidelines) and *moderation*.

Research has documented negative effects of video games on children's physical health. These include obesity; video-induced seizures; and postural, muscular, and skeletal disorders such as tendonitis, nerve compression, and carpal tunnel syndrome. However, these effects are not likely to occur for most children. The research to date suggests that parents should be most concerned about two things: the amount of time that children play and the content of the games that they play.[1]

To address and confront the enormity of this epidemic of deficiency fit kids, the National Football League—to their credit—launched a creative and catchy campaign that would promote educate and encourage fitness for our young people called "PLAY 60" designed to fight childhood obesity.[2]

My generation (baby boomers) was not privy to the degree and level and influence of the electronic, video, computer games that is consequently capturing millions of young people and reducing them to mindless robots that are disengaged and severely suppressed and afflicted with sedentary paralysis. Another consequence of unsupervised game play is that it has produced adult men who have not abdicated their adolescence. Prior to the NFL PLAY 60 program, fun and fitness was not only a premium but it was a common practice and staple for a generation of children.

When I was a kid, we loved being outside, running and ripping out fun being fueled by an imagination that richly enhanced our experience and environment of entertainment and recreation. There was nothing like a good game of cops and robbers, cowboys and Indians, or changing into our DC and Marvel comic heroes at the drop of a hat. We did not need the space shuttle to travel to space. For those of us who had a backyard or woods to play in, it provided the setting and the opportunity to travel to the deepest jungles and rain forests that no soul has ever seen.

To get our heart rate up and our sweat on, we had a blast with red rover, red light-green light, hide and seek, and hopscotch, and we played with every ball in existence. What powered our cars and mode of transportation for play were not batteries but good old body energy and sweat.

For the most part, any activity that we chose to play in a group setting was usually suggested or set by a leader. Someone has to administrate the activity and lead the process. They even decided on the rules and sometimes changed the rules in the middle of the activity. The leader was either self-elected or chosen by the group. For instance, in the game follow-the-leader, everyone obeyed and conformed and copied what the leader did or told us to do. A leader cannot lead without anyone willing to follow him.

This is also true with our faith. If you want to maintain and reclaim personal victory, it is paramount that you embrace and purpose to be loyal to the leadership of the Holy Spirit in your life. It is already established in the Word of God (the Scriptures) that the Holy Spirit is not a force like electricity or even an exercise of emotional influences. He is God—the third party of the Godhead.

The Bible teaches that God is one in essence, three in person: the Father, the Son, and the Holy Spirit (Matthew 3:16-17; 28:19). Each is fully God. God is not three gods but three in one. Although we cannot completely grasp the triune nature of God, we must trust His revelation is true.

By the infinite and immeasurable grace of God, my wife, Gloria, and I have been married for twenty-five years, and Lord willing, it will be three score or more until the Lord calls and catches up His church. Our twenty-five years of marriage has been the richest, most rewarding, and most fulfilling relationship that we ever imagined, hope and dreamed for.

Please, I am not pontificating with pride nor am I promoting a perfect marriage. However, the one that perfects the marriage and prunes our hearts and minds personally and faithfully is the Holy Spirit. I am absolutely certain that the marital relationship will mature, maximize, and move in a majestic measure of blessing and fulfillment. Ultimately and most importantly, a marriage that glorifies God and a marriage where God's witness is established involves two souls that are saturated and submerged in submission. We should submit to the leadership of the Holy Spirit. When He leads, you live. When you lead, you die.

For if ye live after the flesh, ye shall die: but if ye through the *Spirit* do mortify the deeds of the body, ye shall live. (Romans 8:13 KJV, emphasis added)

Our benevolent Father has blessed us with the absolute means and method to mortify, that is put to death the inclinations of iniquity that determine to lead us to separation from God which is death. Consider the matchless modeling of our Master, the Lord Jesus Christ. He submitted to the leadership of the Holy Spirit when He was directed to an unfriendly, isolated, barren, and harsh environment to be tempted by the Devil and for preparation for ministry. Our Lord yielded to the Spirit as opposed to yielding to the temptation.

And Jesus being full of the Holy Ghost returned from Jordan, and was *led* by the Spirit into the wilderness, Being forty days *tempted* of the devil. And in those days he did eat nothing: and when they were ended, he afterward hungered. And the devil said unto him, If thou be the Son of God, command this stone that it be made bread. And Jesus answered him, saying, It is written, That man shall not live by bread alone, but by every word of God. (Luke 4:1-4 KJV, emphasis added)

Did you notice how the Lord overcame the temptation? He stepped on and silenced the screams of selfishness! He submitted to the Holy Spirit. Before you chose to lose in your marriage or as a single surrender to an oversexed society and thereby surrender your purity—whatever the voice of the vice is—*follow the leader.* That is, the leadership of the Holy Spirit. He sustained the Lord and led Him to the Scriptures. The human spirit will lead you to its insidious instincts and failed policies. Depending on natural resources will lead to a world wrecked with ruin.

Conversely, relying on the spiritual resource of the Lord leads to a life that is rich and full in peace and fulfillment. Remember a desperate and depraved and deceitful will always demand submission to his directives, despite the eventual outcome.

Insubordination to the Holy Spirit is indicative of a heart and head that God identifies as "stiff neck." It is a person who purposely pursues their own agenda and is loyal to their self-imposed leadership. Often times an individual may have a complete comprehension of the consequences for not complying with leadership. But they loathe any leadership besides their own. The prophet Jeremiah lobbied for the Lord's leadership among His people. They vociferously rejected his request!

But they obeyed not, neither inclined their ear, but made their neck stiff, that they might not hear, nor receive instruction. Jeremiah 23:17 KJV

A stiff-necked person is totally trapped and taught by a truculent attitude. They trust their own truth, which is not truth but a lie! They are arrested by arrogance, bound by beguilement, and dominated by depravity. This is a heart that loathes the Lord's leadership and loves its own limelight!

Again, when He leads, you live. When you lead, you die and so does everything you touch independent of God— dreams; opportunities; serenity; joy; and purposeful, rich, meaningful, and long-lasting relationships, and a victorious and fulfilled life. An essential component for being willing to follow the leadership of the Holy Spirit is humility.

Discussion Questions

1) Who or what enjoys the greatest influence in your life?
2) What happens when liberties are exercised without restraint and responsibility?
3) What are the things and factors that would cause you to undermine and remove the leadership of the Holy Spirit in your life?
4) Spiritually speaking, what is the cure for a stiff neck?
5) Who will you follow and why?

CHAPTER 8

Harvesting Humility (A Holy Habit)

> Blessed are the poor in spirit:
> for theirs is the kingdom of heaven.
> (Matthew 5:3 KJV)

Harvesting is defined as a supply of anything gathered at maturity and stored. And another word for maturity is *complete*. To create a hostile environment for the flesh and reclaim and maintain personal victory, we must be very proficient at procuring the perfect and complete virtue of humility.

At first glance, the instruction seems to give the impression that I am encouraging a selfish orientation. On the contrary; I endeavor to elucidate the essentiality of this enormous practice that invites the power of God in our lives. Our good God has granted us an incredible invitation to gather in His garden and harvest the heavenly crop of humility. Because its source is divine, it will never be depleted.

Our God embraces and acknowledges a soul that has silenced the voice of self-sufficiency. I submit to you that this is a soul that has substantially secured a sense of one's severe spiritual deficiency. I would like you to ponder the following position: no humility, no heaven. Remember God resists the proud in heart, but He gives grace to the humble. When we seriously saturate our hearts to the submission of God's Spirit and truth, it provides the conditions in the soil of our souls and subsequently the seeds of humility will thrive and flourish as opposed to the seeds of conceit and pride.

Lack of humility will lead to spiritual heart failure. The prideful heart is dominated by demented directives. It produces a heart that is spiritually affected with arteries that are profusely permeated with the plaque and pus of personal pride. Pride that is not purged and eliminated invites permanent punishment from God. Reason with what you are going to read, and hear with your heart what God has said about people who are poisoned by pride: "The wicked, through the pride of his countenance, will not seek after God: God is not in all his thoughts" (Psalm 10:4 KJV).

Pride will always resemble the three-headed monstrosity (FWS) that seeks to mangle us in his mouth. The seeds of humility will never flourish in the hostile environment of hearts heavy in pride. Listen as the Lord's Word gives the perfect and infallible assessment of the human heart condition:

For from within, out of the heart of men, proceed evil thoughts, adulteries, fornications, murders, Thefts, covetousness, wickedness, deceit, lasciviousness, an evil eye, blasphemy, *pride*, foolishness: All these evil things come from within, and defile the man. (Mark 7:21-23 KJV, emphasis added)

The assessment of the human heart or condition did not come from the mental health experts and their board of directors and organizations like the American Psychological Association (APA) Our human condition cannot be accurately assessed by malevolent and misguided magistrates that are moved by FWS (flesh, world, and Satan), or even by liberal clergymen and religious leaders who hold the Word of God in contempt and who professed themselves to be wise. They are indeed fools and are sold out on a profession of profiteering from the flock that the Lord bought with His own blood.

This extraordinary and flawless and superior assessment came from the Lord Almighty. With men and women of faith, the Father will always reject the prideful, but He relishes the humble. He rewards the pride in heart with the wrath that the insolent invited because of their irreverence, but He lavishly pours out an exhaustible resource for grace for the humble.

Likewise, ye younger, submit yourselves unto the elder. Ye, all of you be subject to one another, and be clothed with humility: for God resisteth the proud and giveth grace to the humble. Humble yourselves therefore under the mighty hand of God, that he may exalt you in due time. 1 Peter 5:5-6

God places immense value on all those that serves and loves him. He will pour his immeasurable grace on the humble of heart. Therefore unlike like the inflated (pride) floating device that settles on top of a swimming pool filled with water. We must deflate (humble) ourselves and submerged in his pool of grace and thereby he will surround us with his strength.

Not only can we gather humility, but we also must be dressed in the garment of humility. When we clothe and tie on the garments of humility we will experience the mighty hand of heaven in our lives as opposed to the meager hand of man. Humility takes hold of what I deem as the rule of undiminishing return. The more humility you have, the more grace and goodness will abound in your life: "But he giveth more grace. Wherefore he saith, God resisteth the proud, but giveth grace unto the humble" (James 4:6 KJV).

Paul refers to this anointed attitude as "lowliness of mind" in Philippians 2:3. This heavenly attitude affords us the ability to acknowledge, exalt, and endorse others as opposed to ourselves. This is what harvesting humility looks like. Paul went on to write:

You should enjoy the same mind-set that the Lord Jesus had. We must trace his steps and trace his thoughts in order to gather humility. Let's embrace the Master of humility example, who, being in the form of God, thought it not robbery to be equal with God: But made himself of no reputation, and took upon him the form of a servant, and was made in the likeness of men: And being found in fashion as a man, he humbled himself, and became obedient unto death, even the death of the cross. (Philippians 2:6-8)

When we practice the holy habit of harvesting humility, we gather and store up the power of heaven in our hearts. When we pursue the path of pride, we engage in the power of hell. Harvesting humility is also a mandate from the Master. Without this habit and the power to exercise this habit (the Holy Spirit), you would never be converted or born again. We all have to confess our extreme lost condition and plead for His forgiveness and His righteousness in our lives. Our granite mountain of pride and self-righteousness must be ground to powder. This is true contrition.

The sacrifices of God are a broken spirit: a broken and a contrite heart, O God, thou wilt not despise. (Psalm 51:17 KJV)

God invites us to drink from the eternal fountain of forgiveness and healing waters to quench the flames of personal failure on the condition that we harvest humility.

Discussions Questions

1) How does one develop a holy habit?
2) Why is humility an essential need in your life?

3) How can pride push you away from the most important relationship and push away the power that you need to change?

4) Who is the absolute authority on the human condition and what are His credentials?

5) What has the lack of a humble disposition delivered in your personal life?

CHAPTER 9

A Conscience Captured by Christ (Is Prepared for War)

Casting down imaginations,
and every high thing that exalteth itself against the
knowledge of God, and bringing into captivity every
thought to the obedience of Christ.
(2 Corinthians 10:5 KJV)

As I began to develop this chapter, I was cognizant of the intense conflict between the Spirit of God and our humanity (or the flesh) that is taking place in our hearts and minds. Our bully FWS is intent on invading our hearts and minds. His malignant mission is to establish a filthy fortress of falsehood that would obstruct our view for God. He wants to convince us that he has staked a claim in our conscience and he will not relinquish it.

This war cannot be won with the weapons made by man, but by weapons made by God! When we invoke our intellect, apart from the Spirit of God, we exemplify error and the height of ignorance. It's tantamount to taking toy guns to battle to those who will be using live ammo and real weapons. The apostle Peter admonishes us to be prepared to go to battle at a moment's notice. Do not be caught in a coma of complacency:

Be sober, be vigilant; because your adversary the devil, as a roaring lion, walketh about, seeking whom he may devour: Whom resist stedfast in the faith, knowing that the same afflictions are accomplished in your brethren that are in the world. (1 Peter 5:8-9 KJV)

Whenever I watch lions hunt their prey on the Discovery channel, I have never witnessed them to change their mind and love on a gazelle. With violent force and ferocity, the lions pounce on their prey and clamp on their throats with powerful jaws and pin them to the ground with sharp claws! Likewise, FWS does not come to dance but to dominate, devour, and destroy you: "The thief cometh not, but for to steal, and to kill, and to destroy" (John 10:10a KJV).

The war is not over until the Lord calls us home. Do not turn your sword into plowshares. Don't slumber in self-imposed serenity! To arms, Christian soldiers. Weaponize yourselves with the Lord Jesus Christ. A conscience captured by Christ will never be caught unprepared. Paul gave us our orders from the Lord of Hosts:

Finally, my brethren, be strong in the Lord, and in the power of his might. Put on the whole armour of God, that ye may be able to stand against the wiles of the devil.

For we wrestle not against flesh and blood, but against principalities, against powers, against the rulers of the darkness of this world, against spiritual wickedness in high places. (Ephesians 6:10-12 KJV)

Truth is more lethal and devastating than a nuclear weapon! Truth vaporizes the enemy's lies and strongholds! The truth is powerfully clear! Satan's power over us and his demons was demolished and crushed on the cross of Calvary! The Lord of Heaven with humanity as His uniform destroyed him that had the power of death, the Devil:

Forasmuch then as the children are partakers of flesh and blood, he also himself likewise took part of the same; that through death he might destroy him that had the power of death, that is, the devil; And deliver them who through fear of death were all their lifetime subject to bondage. (Hebrews 2:14-15 KJV)

The Lord's death on the cross and His resurrection decimated the Devil's influence, blew up to pieces his bondage, and thereby canceled out forever his claim in our lives and the captivity that consumed us! Satan abhors all the Scriptures! But if there is a passage that he does not ever want you to discover and believe in order to consistently demolish his schemes and advances, it is this one:

The eyes of your understanding being enlightened; that ye may know what is the hope of his calling, and what the riches of the glory of his inheritance in the saints, And what is the exceeding greatness of his power to us-ward who believe, according to the working of his mighty power, Which he wrought in Christ, when he raised him from the dead, and set him at his own right hand in the heavenly places. (Ephesians 1:18-20 KJV)

My beloved! Let me ask you a question. How much power does it take to raise the dead? Answer: immeasurable, exceeding beyond anything this world has to offer. To assist us in our comprehension, the apostle Paul gave us the picture of the power that raised Christ from the grave! And the authority and that is His at this very moment! Plug into that truth in faith man and women of God! This galvanizing truth will no doubt create a hostile environment in your mind and heart for the flesh. You will maintain and reclaim a dominant personal victory!

We never wage war without the battle gear. Our armor should be on us at all times! It should be just as consistent as our skin. Like a good soldier, we will not get preoccupied and ensnared with the cares and amusements of this life. We should not fall to the world's altar of acceptance or falter for their favor! Hold firm, and when you are under an array of the adversary's assaults, demonic duress, let's embrace and echo to every soldier the Lord orders! Having done all, stand! No matter how unconventional and unpopular your convictions are, stand for the Lord.

Make a commitment to stand in setbacks and dis-appointment of life. Stand when the moral failures of pastors and broken promises from those that you love and respect deeply wound your soul and crush your spirit. Continue to stand in richer or poor, in sickness and health. When the foundations and pillars that made this country strong are disintegrating at a rapid pace and our moral compass is misplaced. Having done all, stand!

Finally, do you have a conscience captured by Christ or captured by Satan's lies? The conscience is defined by one's sense of right or wrong. In the New Testament, the word for *conscience* conveys a moral conscience. Satan seeks to seduce and secure seared consciences. This is accomplished by his deployment of deceitful and deviant demons that deliver their demonic doctrine:

Now the Spirit speaketh expressly, that in the latter times some shall depart from the faith, giving heed to seducing spirits, and doctrines of devils; Speaking lies in hypocrisy; having their conscience seared with a hot iron. (1 Timothy 4:1-2 KJV)

A conscience captured by Christ will violently throw down any attitude, traditions, systems of belief, personal histories, and intangible and tangible things that would cause us to erect idols in our minds and hearts! We do not negotiate with these thoughts; we terminate these thoughts! It is an anointed (Spirit controlled) and assertive mind as opposed to a mind parked in passivity! It is a mind that has been cleaned and purified by the blood of Christ.

Neither by the blood of goats and calves, but by his own blood he entered in once into the holy place, having obtained eternal redemption for us. For if the blood of bulls and of goats, and the ashes of an heifer sprinkling the unclean, sanctifieth to the purifying of the flesh: How much more shall the blood of Christ, who through the eternal Spirit offered himself without spot to God, *purge* your *conscience* from *dead* works to serve the *living* God? (Hebrews 9:12–14 KJV, emphasis added)

A conscience captured by Christ is a conscience that is not dominated by death (serving sin) but is alive and free to serve the Lord.

Discussion Questions

1) Who consistently holds your mind in captivity?
2) Why is it important to weaponize ourselves, and how is this accomplished?
3) Who is the manufacturer of our weapons, and how effective are they?
4) It has been said that you don't take a knife to a gun fight. Spiritually speaking, do you go to war with ineffective weapons?
5) Is your conscience captured by Christ? Why or why not?

CHAPTER 10

The Essentiality of a Christlike Mentality

For who hath known the mind of the Lord, that he may instruct him? But we have the mind of Christ.
(1 Corinthians 2:16 KJV)

Many years ago, officials from the United Negro College Fund employed a provocative advertisement for the purposes to promote education and secure financial support for the outstanding and prestigious legacy of black American colleges: "A mind is a terrible thing to waste."

This is also true for the citizens of the kingdom of God. Too often our perceptions are perverted with the remnants of a rebellious nature. There are occasions that retrospect rewards us with ruin because it is clouded with conceit and confusion. This will cause our Lord's purposes to be pushed downed and trampled by the feet of turmoil.

It is essential that we enjoy a Christ like mentality, because without it we can never comprehend and communicate and change to a conduct that coincides with Christ.

A Christ like mentality is a reality when the Holy Spirit dominates and leads our thoughts. Our preoccupation is not on the terrestrial but on the things that God is concerned with—specifically His will:

If ye then be risen with Christ, seek those things which are above, where Christ sitteth on the right hand of God. Set your affection on things above, not on things on the earth. For ye are dead, and your life is hid with Christ in God. (Colossians 3:1-3 KJV)

Paul reminded us that we were not in the process of procuring the mind of Christ. He emphatically proclaimed we possess the mind of Christ. We believe this by faith which is the power switch to give light to a mind that is darkened by doubt. Feelings, on the other hand, will hold your light switch in the off position. And when the lights are off, you remain in the dark.

Dearly loved of God, we have in our possession the most beautiful mind that ever existed. Because of the Holy Spirit, we can know the positions about what is true and want is right for our lives. We would not have to wear WWJD bands on our wrists because we can know what Jesus would do. With a Christ like mentality, we would know what He would do in any given situation that confronts our paths. When our Lord was on the earth, He was adamant and consistent with this mind-set: "I always do the things that please my Father!" (John 8:29b KJV).

We can only know the things that bring pleasure to our God on the condition that we possess a Christ like mentality. The mind of Christ would be filled by the Spirit and consistently turned to the Scriptures for its authority, answers, actions, and direction. At this juncture, it may be beneficial to define the term *mind* so that we can continue our objective: enjoying the mind of Christ.

The mind is defined as the human consciousness that originates in the brain and is manifested especially in intellect, thought, perception, will, and memory. Biological research suggests that human beings only utilize less than 10 percent of their brain's capacity.

Consider this. It is believed that Albert Einstein, whose theories of relativity revolutionized modern thought, used 10 percent of his brain's capacity. However, a mind that is not mastered by heaven is mastered by the influence of hell. Coincidentally, the fool (an individual who denies the existence of God as well as those who do not subject themselves to His authority) possess an anti-Christ mentality.

There are four positions that characterize the consciousness of a fool:

Fleshly in his thoughts and aspirations
Obeys his passions with the utmost devotion
Outside the will of God for his life
Loses and forfeits forgiveness and eternal life

The fool is indeed the biggest loser: "For what shall it profit a man, if he shall gain the whole world, and lose his own soul?" (Mark 8:36 KJV).

Finally, the anti-Christ mentality is a mind that is

Alienated: It has severed itself from the sanctifying work of God. It is akin to fruit that has fallen on the ground that is decomposing in the dirt. (Ezekiel 23:18)
Carnal: It is a mind dictated by deceit and weakness of humanity. (Romans 8:7)
Doubtful: It is a mind driven by fluctuations, fear, and faithlessness. (Luke 12:29)
Earthly: A mind that is worldly and preoccupied with pleasure. (Philippians 3:19)
Reprobate: Unapproved, worthless, rejected, and judged by God. (Romans 1:28)
Blinded: Minded by Satan and situated in obscurity darkness. (2 Corinthians 4:4)

Conversely, a Christ like mentality is governed and enlightened by the Holy Spirit. It is in harmony with heaven. It exists for the *glory* of God:

Goodness of God
Love of God

Obedience to God
Reverence for God
Yields to the Spirit of God

It is also characterized by the following:

Fellowship: It is in communion and connected to the Spirit of truth. (2 Corinthians 7:7)
Humble: The antithesis of arrogance and pride. (Acts 20:19)
Ready: Available and prepared to take godly action. (Acts 17:11)
Right: A mind that is sound (whole) and serious. (Mark 5:15)
Sound: A mind that is disciplined and self-controlled (managed by the Spirit). (2 Timothy 1:7)
Wise: A man who enjoys a wisdom that comes from the eternal God and not the world. (James 3:15-17)

The Lord God has called us to love Him with all of our mind (Matthew 22:37). The essentiality of a Christ like mentality starts with a good understanding of what the mind is. Here is a tool to train us to monitor, evaluate, and to think with the mind of Christ:

Motivation is the immediate impulse that incites you to take a course of action. Your motivation should compelled by the love of Christ. (2 Corinthians 5:14)
Interest is the degree of concern or attention that is directed to someone or something. For the believer, that

someone should always be Christ first, and that something is His will in your life. (Matthew 6:33)

New birth: It's impossible to possess a Christ like mentality if you are not born from above. We must be born again. The Word of God clearly states that if you do not have His Spirit, you do not belong to Him. (John 3:3; Romans 8:9)

Direction is the management, supervision, and guidance of action or operation of someone or something. Again, that someone is the Lord Jesus Christ, and our direction comes from the Holy Spirit and the inerrant Word of God. (Matthew 4:1; Romans 8:14)

Precious one, a Christ like mentality grants us the power to practice a behavior that brings Him glory. Produce His perspective on life issues and prioritize His purposes for your life and promote a platform of praise to His name!

Discussion Questions

1) What are the signs or symptoms of a mind that is wasting away spiritually?
2) Why is it essential and beneficial to enjoy a Christian mind-set?
3) What steps are needed to enjoy such a mind-set?
4) What are the signs that suggest that you are exercising a fool's mind-set?
5) How do you know if you are loving the Lord Jesus Christ with your mind?

CHAPTER 11

Fixed in the Facts of Freedom

Wherefore lay apart all filthiness and superfluity of naughtiness, and receive with meekness the engrafted word, which is able to save your souls.
James 1:21 KJV

For this chapter, I invite you to entertain the following scenario in order to supplement and secure the steps necessary for creating a hostile environment for your flesh and maintaining or reclaiming personal victory.

Imagine if you will that last evening you elected to redirect your routine behavior. You went to bed earlier than normal because you were not feeling like yourself. You sensed a few slight but not significant symptoms of a cold. You felt a small, scratchy sensation in your throat. Soon you were feeling a little warmer than usual, which seemed to indicate a moderate increase in body temperature. Now you are experiencing a little pressure pressing on both sides of your head. What was an infrequent amount of sneezing has now morphed into moderate mode. So you close your evening by taking a couple of aspirin and flooding yourself with fluids, and you cash in on more vitamin C.

Your preventive measures looked promising and a good night's rest should rebuke any potential storm of sickness—right?

You sought a sweet and sound state of slumber in your warm and inviting bed; however, a maelstrom of sickness motivated with a major degree of malice arrested you in a bed of affliction. Your bed turned into a ship of dread. You were mercilessly being tossed to and fro in mayhem of woe! Terrible torrents of body aches and formidable feverish chills rocked you all night long! Your throat felt like you were trying to swallow a cow! And to compound your complications, a call from the stomach below indicated you were about to blow! You were being nailed by a nasty wave of nausea. By a miracle, you managed to survive the night.

Early before the break of dawn, you called your doctor in hopes that he would deliver you from the devil of a night that you endured. Then you remembered you should have called on Jesus! So then you began to pray that God would smile on you and give you favor and mercy today. You immediately became cognizant that God was moving, because the doctor directed you to come in right away. After the preliminary paperwork and documentation of insurance (another pain), you find yourself in the presence of your professional, personable doctor. Within seconds of his greeting, you hear the standard question: How do you feel?

It's no secret that we are swallowed up by a culture that is overly fixated with how we feel. Addressing our felt needs has become a staple for the solutions of all our issues. Do you feel like coming or going? Do you feel confident? Do you feel capable? Do you feel loved? And one of the most problematic positions on one's assessment is in the area of spirituality: Do you feel like you are going to heaven? Are you free from sin or still held hostage?

When it comes down to our freedom in Christ, we must fix ourselves in the facts of our freedom and not the feel of our freedom. We must flee from feelings and forward ourselves in the firm foundation of God's word by faith. When we place our faith in the facts of our redemption, we will know the truth and experience the freedom that the truth gives:

Then said Jesus to those Jews which believed on him, If ye continue in my word, then are ye my disciples indeed; And ye shall know the truth, and the truth shall make you free. John 8:31-32 KJV

Our Lord is very lucid with the facts! Continue and trust His Word. This is the evidence that leaves no doubt that you are His disciples. You will know and experience the truth about who you are and what has been done in your life with respect to rebellion and bondage. Take note that

He did not say you would feel free but that you will know that you are free.

Again faith in the facts liberates us from our lost condition. Feelings not sanctioned by the Spirit will derail you off the tracks of truth. I mention that because God is not anti-feeling or empty of emotions because He grieves over our sin and He exercises righteous anger when He addresses sin. But most assuredly He also loves, has joy, and smiles on us! My objective is to direct us to the misplacement of feelings that maligns our faith and consequently make us vulnerable to influences that lead us to take courses of action that takes us outside the will of God. The Word of God calls us to walk by faith, live and love by faith, and think with a mind of faith.

It is not what I feel about the truth of God; it is what I know and do with the truth of God, and that will indicate if I have internalized and experienced His freedom in my life. When we fix and plant ourselves in the facts, we will not be moved. Listen to what John says about our eternal salvation. He reminds us that we don't have to guess with our feelings to determine if we are saved; we can know!

He that believeth on the Son of God hath the witness in himself: he that believeth not God hath made him a liar; because he believeth not the record that God gave of his Son. And this is the record, that God hath given to us eternal life, and this life is in his Son. He that hath the Son hath life; and he that hath not the Son of God hath not life. These things have I written unto you that believe on the name of the Son of God; that ye may *know* that ye have eternal life, and that ye may believe on the name of the Son of God. (1 John 5:10-13 KJV, emphasis added)

We are able to exercise an eternal knowledge because the eternal witness—the Holy Spirit—resides in our hearts and mind. We trust the facts about what God has said. We must fix ourselves in the facts.

Feelings that are not sanctioned and submitted to the Spirit are not fixed. They are unstable and always fluctuating and moving. They are akin to clouds. They follow wherever the winds bid them to go. They are not solid, substantive, or eternal like the Scriptures: "Heaven and earth shall pass away, but my words shall not pass away" (Matthew 24:35). "For ever, O LORD, thy word is settled in heaven" (Psalm 119:89).

When we operate in feeling mode as opposed to faith mode, we will be moved by misunderstanding and misery, victimized by vices, and dumped in a ditch of deception and despair. Trusting what we feel will lead us to a treacherous trail thick with turmoil. This leads us to the importance to know what trust is and what trust is not. Trust is the absolute reliance in the CIA: character, integrity, and ability in a person or thing. Who has more CIA than Jesus? There were a number of instances in the Lord's ministry where telling someone just to trust God was initially not received or enough. This happened because they did not have an operational understanding of what they were instructed to do according to the Word of God:

Trust in the Lord with all your heart and lean not to your own understanding. In all your ways acknowledge him and he will direct your path. Proverbs 3:5-6KJV

Wilt thou trust him, because his strength is great? or wilt thou leave thy labour to him? Job 39:11 KJV

God has not called us to try God just as we try on clothing, but to trust God and clothe ourselves in His truth! Sometimes as children of God, we are deficient in our understanding of the call to trust due to the consistent and crippling and crushing of a crisis or storms that assailed us with angry waves of angst and unbelief. It's only natural to find it extremely difficult to fasten ourselves in the truth of trust under the circumstances. However it is important to know that you cannot feel trust. You must forward trust in your mind and heart. By the way, you can never forward what you do not have.

God's Spirit secures the anchor of faith in our hearts that keeps our soul safe and secure while the billows roll, fastened to the rock that cannot be moved, grounded firm and deep in our Savior's love. Now there are five principles that encourage an unadulterated understanding of trust as opposed to a tainted one:

Think
Rest
Understanding
Strength
Truth

Trust starts with how we think. "For as he **thinketh** in his heart, so [is] he" Proverbs 23:7a

If we think with the mind of Christ, that will invite the peace and rest that we need in our hearts and minds. "Thou wilt keep [him] in perfect peace, [whose] mind [is] stayed [on thee]: because he trusteth in thee." Isaiah 26:3; Rest in the LORD, and wait patiently for him: Psalm 37:7a

When we experience the *rest* in our souls, we will then place ourselves in a position to enjoy *understanding*. "For the LORD giveth wisdom: out of his mouth [cometh] knowledge and understanding." Proverbs 2:6

When we have understanding, we also will experience and exercise the strength of the Lord. "The LORD [is] my light and my salvation; whom shall I fear? the LORD [is] the strength of my life; of whom shall I be afraid?" Psalm 27:1

Now that we have the Lord's strength, we can stand in his *truth*! "Sanctify them through thy truth: thy word is truth." John17:17

Trust reveals thoughts that are consistent with the Spirit of God. This leads to rest or peace. How? This powerful progression is possible because your faith has fixed you in the integrity, character, and capacity of the Creator! Trials must be treated with trust. When we navigate through our trials with the compass of trust what will follow are true thoughts serenity and understanding. An unexpected life-changing event will not exempt you from pain. However, because of your decision to think biblically due to the Holy Spirit's influence, you secure serenity and the understanding that will see you through the storm. Subsequently, you will be stabilized by the strength of God and solidified in the truth that "all things work together for good for those that love the God to them that are called according to his purpose" Romans 8:28

When we trust the facts of Scripture, we will be fixed on the path of creating a hostile environment for the flesh and maintaining and reclaiming personal victory in our lives.

Discussion Questions

1) How much of a role do feelings play in framing your perspective in difficult and unpleasant times?
2) How do we deliver ourselves from the relentless and repetitive waves of disquieting emotions?
3) Do you have a faith that is fastened in facts or feelings?
4) What is the difference between trusting God and trying God?
5) Why does God call us to a mandate of faith?

Notes

Chapter 2: Identifying the Bully.
(1)A Mighty Fortress is our God Hymn Site.com.
www.hymnsit.com/lyrics/

Chapter 3: Making a Stand against the Bully
(1)Alexander Woolcott Quotes- Brainy Quote
www.brainyquote.com/quotes/authors/a/alexander_woolcott.
html
(2)Plautus Quotes-Brainy Quote
www.brainyquote.com/quotes/authors/p/plautus.html

Chapter 4: The Arrogance of Self Autonomy
(1)International Humanist and Ethical Union Wikipedia .the free
En.wikipedia.org/wiki/international Humanist and Ethical.
Union

Chapter 5:Meet My Friend MR.MAP
(1)Aristotle Quotes-Brainy Quotes
www.brainyquote.com/quotes/authors/a/aristotle.html
(2)The Winans Songs- Don't Be Decieved Song Lyrics, Music
Video
www.whodatedwho.com The Winans Songs

Chapter 7:The Leadership of the Holy Spirit
(1)The Effects of Video Games on children:What parents need
to know.
www.pedsfor parents.com/articles/279.1shtml
(2)Play 60 NFL Rush
www.nflrusg.com/play60/